The Healthy Oven Baking Book

The
Healthy Oven
Baking Book

Delicious Bake-from-Scratch Desserts
with Less Fat and Lots of Flavor

Sarah Phillips

Doubleday
NewYork London Toronto Sydney Auckland

PUBLISHED BY DOUBLEDAY
a division of Random House, Inc.
1540 Broadway, New York, New York 10036

DOUBLEDAY and the portrayal of an anchor with a dolphin are
trademarks of Doubleday, a division of Random House, Inc.

Healthy Oven is a registered trademark of Healthy Oven, Inc.
Bakes with Applesauce Instead of Butter, Quick-Cake(s), and
Simply Sarah's are all trademarks of Healthy Oven, Inc.

Book design by Ellen Cipriano

Library of Congress Cataloging-in-Publication Data
Phillips, Sarah.
The healthy oven baking book : delicious bake-from-scratch desserts
with less fat and lots of flavor /
Sarah Phillips. — 1st ed.
p.   cm.
Includes index.
1. Baking.   2. Desserts.   3. Low-fat diet—Recipes.
I. Title.
TX763.P437   1999
641.8′15—dc21   98-35411
CIP

ISBN 0-385-49281-2

*This book is dedicated to my family,
and to my late mother, Priscilla. From her I learned
the joys and intricacies of baking and cooking.
I miss her dearly.*

Acknowledgments

To my husband, Reed, and my two children Thomas and Elizabeth (Eswein), and my step-sons, Alex and Zach Phillips, for being such honest taste-testers. Elizabeth was a great help in the kitchen, and Tom was always available to evaluate each and every creation. Alex and Zach were also on hand to give helpful suggestions. This project took two long years, and I couldn't have done it without their support, patience, and encouragement.

To Carol Lloyd, MS Food Science, with whom I have worked closely since 1990, when I first started to develop Healthy Oven Low-Fat Baking Mixes. I interviewed a dozen food scientists before I found Carol, who was the first one who shared my vision for a great-tasting, low-fat baking mix. Her constant technical expertise and advice were indispensable in writing this book.

To Rick Rodgers, the talented cookbook author who helped me get my recipes and thoughts down on paper. I am grateful to him for sharing his knowledge and insights, and for all of his hard work as a recipe tester. And thanks to his two assistants, Diane Kniss and Kelly Volpe. And a special thanks to baker Mäni Niall, for first introducing me to Rick.

To Susan Ginsburg, who became my literary agent, and her assistant John Hodgman, who were always ready to answer my many questions as the book developed from idea to bound copies.

To Judy Kern, my editor, who headed the team to make this book as good as it could be. To Theresa Pulle, assistant, for always being available to answer questions. And to the book's copy editor, Estelle Laurence, whose professionalism and eye for detail was a very important and appreciated part of the process.

To Barbara Duribin, who was responsible for the arduous task of providing the nutritional analysis for each recipe. I know Rick and I tried her patience with our fine tuning, but she never lost her cool.

To my father, Henry Shames, and my late mother, Priscilla Oaks, who believed in me from the start. And to my step-mother, Beverly. Thanks also to my brother Stephen and my sisters Suzanne and Diana for providing me with so many wonderful memories of our antics in the kitchen while we were growing up.

To parents-in-law, Nancy and Reed Phillips Jr., for their trove of old-fashioned family recipes, and for giving me the support to tweak them into The Healthy Oven way of baking.

Finally, to the pastry professor at the Culinary Institute of America, who took me aside one day and said that I should go into the food business. I don't remember his name, but his advice certainly stuck.

Contents

· ❋ ·

In a Flash: Quick Breads and Cakes

New Cake Classics: Layer Cakes and Cheesecakes for Special Occasions with Frostings, Glazes, and Sauces — 101

The New Pie Cupboard: Pies, Tarts, and Other Pastries

From the Cookie Jar: Bars, Cookies, and Brownies

The Healthy Oven Baking Book

Introduction

About Healthy Oven

he *Healthy Oven Baking Book* is a complete how-to-bake cookbook with over 125 recipes. Most of the recipes are made with applesauce instead of butter. The others use foolproof techniques to reduce the fat, but all of the finished recipes will be hard to distinguish from the classic, fat-packed versions of your favorite desserts. As an added bonus to their healthy profiles, the vast majority of these recipes can be ready for the oven in under ten minutes. When developing the recipes, I kept busy cooks like myself in mind, and used common pan sizes and simple baking techniques. I also made sure that when analyzing these recipes for their nutritional content (including calories, fat, and cholesterol), I used realistic portions based on what my family eats. I have personally tested and retested these recipes many times to be certain that even beginning bakers could make them without any problems. Fast, easy, and healthful—that's a pretty powerful combination!

Since 1993, my Healthy Oven Low-Fat Baking Mixes (that "Bake with Applesauce Instead of Butter") have been available at supermarkets and natural food stores across the nation, and by mail-order, too. These all-natural muffin and cake mixes speak directly to today's cooks, who are increasingly concerned about a healthy diet. Although baking mixes are my bread and butter—pun intended—and I have included a few recipes that use them, this is a "from scratch" cookbook.

People always ask me how I started my business, and the answer is simple: I thought of the way my family eats, saw a hole in the market, and filled it. Luckily, I had been preparing for this job for years. I just didn't know it. My mom was a great baker, and I learned to bake at an early age. (Growing up in California around fresh fruits and vegetables and the organic food movement didn't hurt, either.) Throughout college, I honed my skills as a home baker, concentrating on icons of the seventies' kitchen like carrot cake and zucchini bread. But, as much as I loved baking, I had to pay the bills, and worked in sales at a financial consulting firm. After a tough day of selling financial software, I retreated into the kitchen as soon as I got home. On weekends and evenings, I squeezed in baking classes around my responsibilities as a mother. All of a sudden, I became a casualty of corporate downsizing. Then my marriage broke up, and I found myself in the challenging position of being an unemployed single parent with two children.

The plucky woman who pulls herself up by her apron strings instead of her bootstraps has become a cultural cliché, but in my case, it is all true. I obtained a license to bake out of my home, and I started a line of all-natural cookies called Simply Sarah's. They were a hit, and I learned a lot about the Manhattan gourmet jungle. If you think baking tray after tray of cookies in your home kitchen with two youngsters running around sounds like a lot of work (not to mention the packing, delivery, and marketing of said cookies), you're right! Even though I loved the creative part of the business, I knew it was time for change . . . again. Because I already knew the buyers at the top-end markets, I found a job with the perfect fit: a sales representative for a leading food distributor, selling some of the best all-natural food products around.

Throughout this period, I was still a mom, faced with making bag lunches for my kids. Like most busy parents, I turned to convenience foods to help in the kitchen. But, when I looked at the nutritional and ingredients labels, I put the boxes back on the shelves. Some of them had so many chemicals they looked more like formulas for rocket fuel than recipes. My family loved my homemade, old-fashioned applesauce muffins, but I felt the time had come for all of us to watch our fat intake. So, I experimented with reducing the fat in the recipe, and it took me months to get it just right. I sent the new, improved home-baked muffins to school in the kids' lunch boxes. The next thing I knew, my kids starting asking for extra muffins to share with their buddies, and then came phone calls from the parents asking where they could buy the muffins their kids were raving about. When I told them they were homemade, *and* low-fat, *and* made with all-natural ingredients, they convinced me I was onto something big.

I immersed myself in developing my own Healthy Oven muffin mixes. I saw no reason to load my mixes with preservatives and chemicals. Instead of large amounts of shortening used by most mixes, mine would use applesauce (an ingredient that low-fat bakers know they can substitute for fats in many baked goods), egg white powder as a convenience to the baker so they don't have to use fresh, and a minimum of oil. Working from small batches with all-natural ingredients, my first muffin mix flavors were Cinnamon, Chocolate, Ginger, and Orange. Then came Quick-Cake mixes in Apple-Cinnamon, Chocolate, Lemon, and Pumpkin-Orange. Eventually, I left my job to concentrate on the Healthy Oven line. To be in close contact with my customers' needs, I established a newsletter, a web site, and an e-mail address. National food magazines ran great reviews of the mixes. I appeared on television making muffins. And now, this cookbook.

Low-fat baking is different from conventional baking. Fat forms the backbone of most old-fashioned baking recipes, and when the fat is reduced or eliminated, there is a whole new set of rules. I learned low-fat baking the hard way, by trial and error. I want to share my experiences, but with more than just recipes. This book explains not only the ingredients that make tasty healthful desserts but also the techniques that guarantee success. The modern baker who wants a low-fat dessert must approach the recipe with a new sensibility. Once you have made a recipe or two, the new low-fat baking techniques will become second nature, just as the old methods were.

Even though this book teaches how to make mouthwatering healthful desserts, it is not a "diet" cookbook. I'm not going to get on my soapbox and lecture about the benefits of a low-fat daily diet. It would be preaching to the choir. (After all, you picked this book up because you already have some interest in the subject, and the media hasn't exactly neglected the issue.) Suffice it to say that if you restrict the fat in your diet, you reduce your chances of heart disease, stroke, and certain forms of cancer. And you won't look so bad, either! Most health experts recommend that your diet derive no more than 30 percent of its daily calorie intake from fat, and some doctors feel that 25 percent or even lower is ideal.

However, some people have gone overboard in their zeal to trim the fat from their food. Especially with baked goods, if you take out *too* much fat, you end up with something that resembles a dessert, but not something that most people would call delicious. The success of my company is based on the premise that our cakes and muffins don't taste or look "low-fat," even though they fit the FDA specifications. (The mixes are no-fat, and I ask you to add a minimum of canola oil as a flavor conservator, along with applesauce and water.) In general, it is more helpful to count the number of fat grams consumed over a couple of days than to be on the constant lookout to eliminate any foods that get over 30 percent of their calories from fat. (Check with your doctor or a dietitian to find out the recommended amount of fat grams for your age and height and desired weight. It averages around 50 grams per day for women, and 60 grams per day for men.) Sometimes a dessert will be a few percentage points over 30 percent. That doesn't mean you shouldn't eat it. It means that I have removed as much fat as possible, and that my testing showed that if I cut the fat any further, the results were not as good. Remember that balance plays a big part in any food plan—a piece of ripe, fresh fruit is just as much a dessert as a low-fat brownie. Also, few people maintain a healthy lifestyle without exercise.

The Healthy Oven Baking Book shows you how to use new techniques to get old-fashioned results. For me, it's not enough that a dessert has a reduced-fat profile—it has to taste delicious, too. I am often discouraged when I try low-fat desserts that aren't so wonderful, because I know how good they can really be. Here's an array of sumptuous layer cakes, crisp cookies, fudgy brownies, fruity pies and tarts, creamy cheesecakes, homespun muffins, and golden-brown quick breads that are so tasty they will receive the ultimate compliment: No one will suspect that they are low-fat. I am especially thrilled with the innovative, luscious, reduced-fat frosting recipes that I developed at the urging of the many customers who asked me for guilt-free icings for their trimmed-down cakes.

While this is essentially a book of recipes, I think it is important for bakers to understand *why* certain ingredients and techniques work. A detailed explanation of how low-fat baking works and concise instructions for the most common techniques can be found in The Healthy Oven Basics section that begins on page 8. If you are an experienced baker, and you want to move ahead to the recipes, fine . . . but, I encourage you to read this section before you start.

Now that I have learned the essentials of successful low-fat baking, I want to teach them to you. I hardly ever make any of my old recipes anymore, having adjusted them to fit a healthier profile. I hope that this book gives you a whole trove of new recipes, shows you how to become a new kind of baker, and inspires you to transform your own old recipes into low-fat delights.

Sarah Phillips
e-mail: healthyovn@aol.com
web site: http://www.healthyoven.com

What the Numbers Mean . . .

*E*very recipe in this book has been analyzed for its nutritional content. Most of the recipes fall within the U.S. Food and Drug Administration's specifications for low-fat, low-saturated fat, low-sodium, and low-cholesterol foods. The remaining recipes (usually for frosted cakes or pies), fall into the reduced-fat category. Even though the USFDA's terms and serving sizes are designed for grocery labels, they have become such a part of our food language that you can apply them to the recipes in this book, as well. Here's what these specifications mean:

Fat-free	Fewer than 0.5 grams per serving
Low-fat	3 grams or less per serving
Low-saturated fat	1 gram or less per serving
Low-sodium	140 milligrams or less per serving
Low-cholesterol	20 milligrams or less, and 2 grams or less of saturated fat per serving
Lean	Fewer than 10 grams of fat, 4.5 grams or less of saturated fat, and less than 95 milligrams of cholesterol
Reduced	Contains at least 25 percent less of an ingredient (such as sodium or fat) than the regular version

The Nutritional Analyses in this book list the percentage of calories derived from fat, because the USFDA also recommends that it be no more than 30 percent, with no more than 10 percent from saturated fat. Keep in mind that this recommendation applies to the total diet, not just individual recipes, and should be calculated over a period of days. You will also find the percentages of calories derived from carbohydrates and protein for each recipe. All of the percentages have been rounded to the nearest number, so they may not always add up to exactly 100 percent.

The Healthy Oven Basics

erhaps the best way to illustrate how reduced-fat baking works is to tell the story of how I gave my mom's chocolate fudge cake a makeover (see Chocolate Fudge Layer Cake (page 110) with Fudgy Chocolate Frosting on page 133). It didn't happen overnight.

I have vivid memories of Mom in the kitchen, instinctively mixing up her famous chocolate fudge cake in a big bowl. She made it so many times, she never had to look at the recipe. I learned it by heart, too: two sticks of butter, two cups of sugar, two whole eggs (Mom preferred double-yolk), one-half cup of sour cream, two cups of sifted all-purpose flour, three ounces of unsweetened chocolate, one cup of hot brewed coffee, one teaspoon of baking soda, and a pinch of salt. The frosting had four more ounces of chocolate, one pound of confectioners' sugar, and one teaspoon of vanilla, mixed with a whole raw egg (I doubt if she'd use a raw egg today) and a few tablespoons of whole milk.

When my family decided to pay more attention to our diet, I knew that Mom's chocolate fudge cake, as it stood, didn't fit into the plan—especially after I ran the numbers on the original recipe. I almost fainted when the calculations showed 603 calories, 28 fat grams (11 grams of saturated fat), and 100 milligrams of cholesterol *per slice* (twelve slices per cake)! If I had announced to my gang that they would never eat chocolate cake again, they would have packed their bags and found a new mom and wife. But I knew that somewhere in Mom's beloved recipe there was a wonderful reduced-fat version just waiting to be discovered.

So, I rolled up my sleeves and got busy. Obviously, the place to start was with the butter. Fat serves several purposes in a baked good, primarily contributing to and enhancing the flavor. After much experimentation, I found that I could cut the fat down from sixteen to four tablespoons—25 percent of its original amount—before the flavor and texture were adversely affected. (In other recipes, substituting a fruit puree like applesauce for part of the fat works well.) I also substituted low-gluten cake flour for the all-purpose flour, as cake flour will produce a more tender cake, which can be a problem in the absence of fat.

To make up for the flavor lost by reducing the amount of the melted chocolate, I added one-half cup of cocoa powder, which is a surprisingly low-fat ingredient. In addition I added two teaspoons of instant espresso to complement the chocolate flavor. I used low-fat buttermilk which has a similar full, rich flavor to sour cream, but fewer calories and less fat.

Egg yolks provide fat and lecithin (a natural emulsifier), which contribute to the fine texture of baked goods, and egg whites contain proteins that give structure to the final product. I could have substituted four egg whites for the two whole eggs, but I kept one egg and substituted two whites for the other. The little bit of lecithin in that one yolk made a big difference. Too many egg whites will make a baked good dry and rubbery.

Finally, I added an important instruction to the recipe: "Do not open the oven until the last five minutes of baking." All low-fat and reduced-fat baked goods are extremely sensitive to shifts in oven temperature, which occur when the door is opened, and could fall.

Of course, I didn't get it right on the first try. But, get it right I did, because I came to understand the interplay between the ingredients and the techniques used in reduced-fat baked goods. And finally, after many trials, I came up with a rich, delicious, chocolate cake and a new fudgy frosting that my family loves. This Chocolate Fudge Layer Cake (page 110), with the Fudgy Chocolate Frosting (page 133), was reduced by over 280 calories, 18 grams fat (6 grams saturated fat), and 69 mg cholesterol, per piece!

How Low-Fat Baking Works

The rules for low-fat baking are completely different from those for traditional full-fat baking. Reduced- and low-fat batters are more sensitive to over-mixing, overbaking, ingredient substitutions, improper measuring, oven temperatures, and choice of baking pans. Practically every baked good, traditional or reduced-fat, is created from a balance of many components. A recipe is a culinary formula. Each component has a role to play in the formula and the success of the final result. It is important that the baker understands how these ingredients work, and why they require different mixing and baking methods than the ones my mom taught me when I was first learning my way around the kitchen.

For example, most of Mom's recipes start with a large amount of butter, which, through creaming with crystalline sugar, creates and traps air and moisture in the batter. In reduced-fat baking, the butter is significantly reduced or eliminated altogether, and the fat is often replaced by a fruit puree and other ingredients. If butter is used at all, it is as a flavoring.

Here are the basic components that you'll find in almost every recipe for any baked good.

Strengtheners: Wheat flours and egg whites contain proteins that provide strength for a batter or dough so it will rise and not collapse when baked. When wheat flour is moistened and stirred, two proteins in the flour, glutenin and gliadin, connect and cross-connect to form strands of gluten, which help give structure to the baked good. Wheat is the only grain with significant amounts of gluten-forming potential. Other grains like corn and oats, and therefore products like cornmeal and oatmeal, do not create gluten in a batter. They provide only flavor and bulk, and must be mixed with wheat flour for strength.

Depending on the type of wheat and where and when it was planted, the resulting flour can be high-gluten (milled from hard winter wheat), low-gluten (from soft spring wheat), or moderate (a combination of the two). Baked goods made from high-gluten flours have a firm crumb; low-gluten flours give more tender results, and goods made from flours with a moderate gluten content fall somewhere in between.

The more a batter is stirred, the stronger the gluten becomes. Fat, which is not present in reduced-fat baking in traditional amounts, plays an important role in coating the proteins in flour, minimizing their contact with moisture, and shortening the gluten's development. Without the fat lubricator, the gluten strands form more readily. That is why it is very important never to overmix a reduced-fat batter. You'll see the phrase "Do not overmix" in practically every recipe in this book.

I often use unbleached all-purpose flour, which has a moderate gluten content. For a lower gluten content with a more tender outcome, I use whole wheat *pastry* flour or cake flour. In a few cases, I also use high-gluten, regular whole wheat flour. Each recipe is written with a specific flour in mind to give the best results.

Shortening (Fats): Most bakers are very familiar with traditional shortenings such as butter, margarine, and vegetable shortening. Shortenings coat the flour proteins, reducing their contact with the moisture in the recipe, and shortening the length of the gluten strands when the flour is stirred with that moisture (that's why they're called "shortenings"). In traditional baking, where solid fats are creamed with crystalline sugar, tiny air cells are whipped into the batter, so the baked good will have a fine, aerated texture. When a shortener is removed or reduced, it increases the chances that the end product will lack flavor and be tough and full of tunnels. The new mixing methods in this book reduce this possibility. Butter makes a very important flavor contribution, whereas margarine does not have as fine a texture and taste, so when choosing a shortening, I always go for the butter, but in the small amounts that are needed to retain a great taste and aroma. If you have dietary restrictions that make it necessary for you to reduce saturated fats in your diet, you can substitute a butter-margarine blend (see page 252). The recipe won't taste the same if you use margarine.

Vegetable oil does not act as a shortener because it is a liquid and won't cream with crystalline sugar in the same way as a solid fat. It reduces dryness and enhances flavor, so I use it sparingly because it has the same number of calories and fat grams as butter, even though it has less saturated fat.

Fat Substitutes (Fruit Purees): Fruit purees, especially applesauce, are often used as fat substitutes. The pectin from the fruit forms a film around the tiny air bubbles in the batter, similar to what occurs when you cream solid shortenings with sugar, but not as effectively.

My favorite fruit puree for baking is unsweetened applesauce. Not only is it readily available but it is inexpensive and versatile because it doesn't impart any strong flavor to the final result. Applesauce contains more pectin than other fruit purees, which helps to retain the moistness of baked goods. Even if a recipe is flavored with another fruit puree, I always add a little applesauce as well.

You'll see recipes here that use pumpkin, banana, and prune purees, among others.

Sweeteners: Sugars provide sweetness and flavor. Crystalline sugars, such as granulated white sugar and brown sugar, are integral to the creaming process that incorporates air into batters. Sugar also inhibits gluten formation, which means that sugar helps make baked goods tender. Honey and corn syrup are liquid sweeteners, and while they do provide sweetness, they do not cream well, just as liquid vegetable oils can't substitute for solid shortenings.

Leaveners: Most desserts are leavened with baking soda or baking powder, or by the air beaten into egg whites. (Yeast, not used in this book also makes baked goods rise.)

Baking soda (bicarbonate of soda) is alkaline. When it comes in contact with an acidic ingredient like applesauce, buttermilk, or lemon juice and is moistened, the alkali/acid combination creates carbon dioxide. This carbon dioxide expands the air bubbles previously formed by creaming, and makes the baked good rise. In some recipes, depending on the quantity of acidic ingredients included, a combination of baking soda and baking powder is used for better flavor and texture.

Baking powder does not need an acidic ingredient to release its leavening power. Double-acting baking powder begins releasing carbon dioxide as soon as it is moistened, and again when heated in the oven. Some baking powders include sodium aluminum sulfate, but there are aluminum-free baking powders that work just as well, and I prefer them. Look for a brand like Rumford's at natural food stores or many supermarkets.

When egg whites have air beaten into them, they also act as a leavening. In most reduced-fat recipes, one or two egg whites are beaten with sugar and other ingredients to make a frothy liquid covered with tiny air bubbles. This is very different from the twelve egg whites beaten to the soft- or stiff-peak stage that are folded into regular batters (although Orange Angel Food Cake, on page 102, based on the low-fat classic, depends on stiff whites for its light-as-a-feather texture).

Thickeners: Not every recipe includes a thickener, although flour certainly has thickening attributes. But many fruit fillings include cornstarch to thicken the juices. I occasionally use tapioca as a thickener, as well.

Flavorings: Flavorings enhance a baked good's aroma and taste. The butter in traditional recipes contributes to and carries flavors throughout the batter. Even more important, butter has flavor of its own that, when it interacts with sugar, is responsible for the caramelized baked taste we associate with baked goods. In reduced-fat baking, the flavorings must be increased to compensate for the reduction in butter.

Steps to Successful Low-Fat Baking

There are a few familiar baking procedures that are a bit different in reduced-fat baking. Use these techniques when preparing the recipes in this book, and you'll have success every time.

Measuring: All of the flour in this book has been measured by the spoon-and-sweep method. This method is becoming a common low-fat technique and many food magazines, such as *Cooking Light*, use it. Flour settles, and can compact itself in its bag in the long journey from the mill to the grocer to your home. In order to give your baked goods a nice, light crumb, the flour must be aerated. The best place to start is when the flour is measured. If you measure the flour with the scoop-and-sweep method (by dipping the cup into the bag and sweeping the excess flour off the top with a knife), you will be baking with compacted flour, and you could end up with a dense, dry baked good.

It's so important to remind you of the spoon-and-sweep measuring method, that I have stated the procedure next to every flour measurement in the book. I once calculated the difference in weight between one cup of spooned and one cup of scooped whole wheat pastry flour. It was almost an ounce, which is 20 percent! That will make quite a big difference in the final taste and texture of the recipe.

To measure by the spoon-and-sweep method, place the dry measuring cup on a plate or a piece of waxed paper (to catch the excess flour). Using a large spoon, stir the flour in the bag or container, and lightly spoon it into the cup until it overflows. Do not pack the flour in the cup. Using a knife (or even your finger), sweep off the excess flour so it is level with the top of the cup. Cocoa can be lumpy unless sifted. In that case, measure the cocoa and sift it. It is fine to measure the other dry ingredients in the book by scooping, as long as you use level measures.

Always use metal measuring cups for dry ingredients, and a glass measuring cup for liquid ingredients. For dense, moist ingredients, such as applesauce, peanut butter, and yogurt, use level amounts in a metal measuring cup. When measuring buttermilk and sticky liquid ingredients like corn syrup, molasses, or honey, place the glass measuring cup on a work surface, and measure the liquid at eye level. Don't hold the glass up in the air, or you can make an inaccurate measure. To help remove sticky liquids from the measure, spray the inside with nonstick canola oil spray before measuring. Be sure to scrape all of the ingredient out of the measure with a rubber spatula.

Nonstick Baking Pans: To reduce sticking, always use nonstick pans and muffin tins sprayed with canola or vegetable oil spray. Low-fat batters especially stick to the surfaces of regular baking pans without a nonstick lining. In that case, generously spray with oil. Do not use disposable aluminum foil pans, which absorb the oven heat unevenly and have hot spots. To be sure that your cake unmolds easily from the pan, optionally line the bottom of a nonstick pan with a piece of waxed or parchment paper. Generally, I don't recommend paper muffin liners, as some batters stick to them no matter what you do. If you use them, spray the insides of the liners with oil.

Try to use nonstick insulated cookie sheets—they encourage even browning much better than the regular sheets. Lightly spray with oil. You can simulate these double-thick sheets by stacking one regular cookie sheet inside another. If your sheets don't have a nonstick coating, generously spray or line the pans with waxed paper or baking parchment (no need to spray the parchment paper).

I prefer ovenproof glass pie plates. They distribute the heat better than metal ones, and you can look underneath to see how the crust is browning. I also prefer ovenproof glass pans for fruit-based desserts, but you can use nonstick metal ones, as well. Although glass manufacturers recommend reducing the oven temperature by 25° F when using their products, I never do it, and my pies and fruit desserts always turn out fine. Generously spray any ovenproof glass pans with oil.

Mixing: Even though all these recipes can be mixed by hand, I use a KitchenAid portable electric mixer to whip the liquid ingredients into a froth. Almost everyone has one. (The volume of liquid ingredients is too shallow for the beaters of a heavy-duty standing mixer to work properly.) Never use an electric mixer to mix in the flour. It will overdevelop the gluten, and toughen the baked good. Always stir in the flour with a spoon, just enough to moisten.

Preheating the Oven: In any kind of baking, a properly preheated oven is a key to success. It usually takes about twenty minutes for an oven to reach the desired temperature, so be sure to allow enough time. Always double-check the oven temperature with a free-standing oven thermometer. Never believe the temperature on your thermostat dial—these thermostats are notoriously unreliable.

The position of the rack is another important point. Before turning on the oven, adjust the rack to the position designated in the recipe. Heat rises, and if a cake, for example, is baked in the top third of the oven, it will brown, and possibly burn, more quickly than one baked in the center rack.

Some pastry recipes require a pie to be baked on a baking sheet (it doesn't have to be nonstick) in the lower third of the oven. In a gas oven, this places the pie plate nearest the source of heat. In an electric oven, place the sheet in the center rack. You don't want the baked good to be too close to the heat source, or it will burn. The hot baking sheet gives the pie dough a flat, solid surface to bake on, which promotes an evenly browned, crisp crust and catches any drips.

When making regular cookies, some people bake two sheets at a time, switching the position of the sheets halfway through baking. This doesn't work with reduced-fat cookies, as the hot air should be encouraged to circulate to brown the cookies evenly, and the second sheet blocks the circulation. Bake cookies one sheet at a time, in the center of the oven. If you have only one baking sheet, line it with parchment paper so you can move quickly to the second batch without having to wash the sheet. However, the sheet should be cooled before using it again. Don't cool cookie sheets by rinsing them under cold water, or they could warp.

Doneness: Watch out for overbaking! It's a major cause of low-fat baking failures, whether you are baking cakes, cookies, or quick breads. Low-fat baked goods may have moist, shiny tops and *look* underdone, but those looks can be deceiving.

Low-fat cake baking has a different set of doneness tests from traditional baking. In full-fat baking, the most common method of testing for doneness is to insert a toothpick or a thin wire cake tester into the center of the cake. If the toothpick comes out clean, without any unbaked batter clinging to it, the cake is done. The toothpick test doesn't work with reduced-fat baking, which requires other visual and tactile tests to be sure the baked good is baked through. This also holds for muffins and quick breads.

1. To avoid overbaking, check for doneness at the beginning of the specified time range.
2. Unless specified in the recipe, the top will spring back when gently pressed in the center.
3. The edges are lightly browned and are beginning to pull away from the sides of the pan. Some quick breads will develop a large crack running down the top—it's normal.

Bake cookies until they are very lightly browned around the edges. The centers may seem underdone, but they will firm upon cooling. If the cookies cool and harden onto the sheet, return the sheet to the oven for a few seconds or so until the cookies soften (they won't stick to nonstick sheets).

Pie crusts should be baked until golden brown. If a pie crust is over-browning before the filling is done (the center should jiggle only slightly when the pie is shaken), protect the crust by covering it with strips of aluminum foil.

Cooling: Some baked goods are meant to be eaten right out of the pan, and can be cooled in the pan on a wire cake rack. For cake and loaf recipes that require unmolding, place the pan on a wire cake rack and let it stand for 10 minutes. Run a knife around the inside of the pan to release the cake from the sides, then invert it onto the rack. If the loaf pan has been lined with waxed paper, carefully peel it off the loaf. Turn the loaf right side up and cool completely on the rack. A few cakes and quick breads may sink slightly in the center when cooled. When they are sliced, the indentation won't be so noticeable, so don't worry about it. Cool cookies on a wire cake rack.

Storage: Most reduced-fat baked goods will keep for up to two days at room temperature, wrapped in aluminum foil. Foil works better than plastic wrap or plastic bags, which hold in the moisture. (Because of the moisture-attracting properties of fruit purees, low-fat baked goods can "sweat.") However, cookies keep best in zip-tight plastic bags. You can refrigerate the baked goods if you wish, but most of them are best if served at room temperature. Well wrapped in aluminum foil and placed in a zip-tight bag, they can also be frozen for up to two months. Always cool baked goods completely before storing. Store all frosted cakes, cheesecakes, and pies in the refrigerator.

The New Techniques

There are two methods used most often in this book. They are the New Classic Method and the New Creaming Method. With either method, the goal is to evenly distribute the leavening and other ingredients throughout the batter for better volume, to create air bubbles, and to develop minimum gluten so that the baked good will be tender and full of flavor. In other words, to make a low-fat dessert that is simply delicious.

Even though each recipe includes a thorough, detailed explanation of each method, reading about them beforehand will help familiarize the baker with new procedures. If a recipe uses one of the two new methods, I have designated it, so you can turn to these pages for a step-by-step reference. In the ingredients list for each recipe, the components in each step are separated to emphasize the fact that they are mixed differently from the way they might be in traditional recipes.

The New Classic Method: Everything in this method is done to avoid overmixing, which develops the gluten and toughens the baked good, and to incorporate air into the batter. Follow these steps for tender, moist cakes, quick breads, and muffins where the traditional shorteners have been replaced by fruit purees. The batter uses two mixing bowls: one for dry ingredients and a second for the liquids and sugar. The liquids and sugar are beaten until frothy, then poured into the dry ingredients and gently stirred into a batter.

1. *Preheat* the oven, positioning the rack as instructed in the recipe.

2. *Prepare* any baking pans by spraying with canola or vegetable oil spray.

3. *Whisk* the dry ingredients (except the sugar) in the first mixing

bowl until well combined and aerated. If the mixture includes cocoa, and seems lumpy, you may have to sift it. Set it aside.

4. *Beat* the liquid ingredients (including the sugar) with a handheld electric mixer beginning on a low speed to avoid spattering. Then quickly increase the speed to high for $1^{1}/_{2}$ to 2 minutes until the mixture is frothy, with tiny air bubbles on the surface. You can also briskly whisk the mixture to get the same result. Make a well in the center of the dry ingredients, and pour in the liquids.

5. *Stir* the flour and liquid ingredients with a spoon (never with a mixer) just until combined. Work quickly and do not overmix. The gluten begins to develop as soon as the flour is moistened and stirred. If adding other ingredients, such as raisins, stir the batter just until moistened, with a few traces of flour remaining. Add the ingredient, and gently fold it in until the flour is incorporated. Unless indicated otherwise, the batter will be somewhat thick. Don't worry if it is slightly lumpy.

6. *Transfer* the batter to the prepared pan, handling it gently so the batter doesn't deflate. If the top needs to be smoothed with a rubber spatula, use a gentle touch.

7. *Bake* just until the cake tests done (see page 16). Do not overbake, or the baked good will be dry and flavorless.

8. *Cool* on a wire cake rack for 10 minutes before removing from the pan to cool completely on the rack, or to serve directly from pan, as indicated.

The New Creaming Method: This is the reduced-fat method for mixing all kinds of cookies and butter-based cakes. Creaming usually means to beat room-temperature butter (or some other shortening fat) with crystalline sugar until the mixture is light in color and somewhat fluffy in texture. This procedure beats air into the butter/sugar combination, giving the batter an aerated base on which to build. With the amount of butter reduced, the aeration doesn't take place as effectively. In this case, the butter is used more as a flavoring than as a base, but you still need to cream the reduced amount of butter with the sugar.

1. *Preheat* the oven, positioning the rack as instructed in the recipe.

2. *Prepare* any baking pans by spraying with canola or vegetable oil spray.

3. *Whisk* the dry ingredients (except the sugar) in the first mixing bowl until well combined and aerated. (Cocoa may need to be sifted to eliminate lumps.)

4. *Combine* the butter (cut into small pieces and at room temperature) with the sugar in a 1-quart glass measuring cup or a deep-sided medium bowl. The depth of the measuring cup helps the butter and sugar to mix better than in a regular bowl. I also like to "start" the butter/sugar mixture by rubbing the two ingredients together with my fingertips until they form a well-mixed mass. Using a handheld electric mixer set at high speed, mix thoroughly, scraping down the sides of the bowl often with a rubber spatula, until the mixture is light in color and resembles coarse bread crumbs, about 2 minutes. The mixture will not become "light and fluffy" as described in traditional recipes.

5. *Beat* the liquid ingredients in another bowl with the electric mixer just until combined. The mixture does not have to get frothy. Pour it into the butter/sugar mixture and beat on low speed just until combined.

6. *Add* the flour mixture and stir with a spoon, just until mixed. Do not overmix. If adding other ingredients, such as raisins, stir the batter just until moistened with a few traces of flour remaining. Add the ingredient, and gently fold it in until the flour is incorporated. Don't worry if the batter is slightly lumpy.

7. If making a cake, *transfer* the batter to the prepared pan, handling it gently so the batter doesn't deflate. If the top needs to be smoothed with a rubber spatula, use a gentle touch. If making cookies, transfer the dough to the prepared cookie sheets according to the recipe directions.

8. *Bake* just until the cake tests done or the cookies are lightly browned around the edges. Do not overbake, or the fat-reduced batter could become dry and flavorless.

9. *Cool* cakes on a wire cake rack for 10 minutes before removing from the pan to cool completely or to serve directly from the pan, as indicated. Cool cookies on the sheets for a few minutes before transferring them to wire cake racks to cool completely.

Stirring Up Trouble . . .

Some of these recipes are purposely plain, so you can add whatever you have on hand to personalize the final result. But sometimes that creative touch can also add too many fat grams and calories. Nuts, for example, add a lot of flavor and crunch, but the fat grams can sneak up on you. To calculate the amount of fat grams and/or calories per serving, just divide the number of servings in the recipe, and add the figures on. All amounts are for 1/2 cup.

Chocolate chips	18 fat grams	400 calories
Walnuts, chopped	35 fat grams	380 calories
Pecans, chopped	40 fat grams	397 calories
Hazelnuts, chopped	36 fat grams	364 calories
Macadamia nuts	49 fat grams	470 calories
Cashews, halved	32 fat grams	395 calories
Almonds, slivered	35 fat grams	398 calories
Pumpkin seeds	6 fat grams	143 calories
Sweetened coconut flakes	12 fat grams	143 calories
Raisins	0 fat grams	290 calories
Dried cranberries	less than 1 fat gram	182 calories
Dried cherries	less than 1 fat gram	182 calories
Dried apples	less than 1 fat gram	105 calories
Chopped pitted dates	0 fat grams	280 calories

Rise and Shine: Coffee Cakes, Muffins, and Other Breakfast Treats

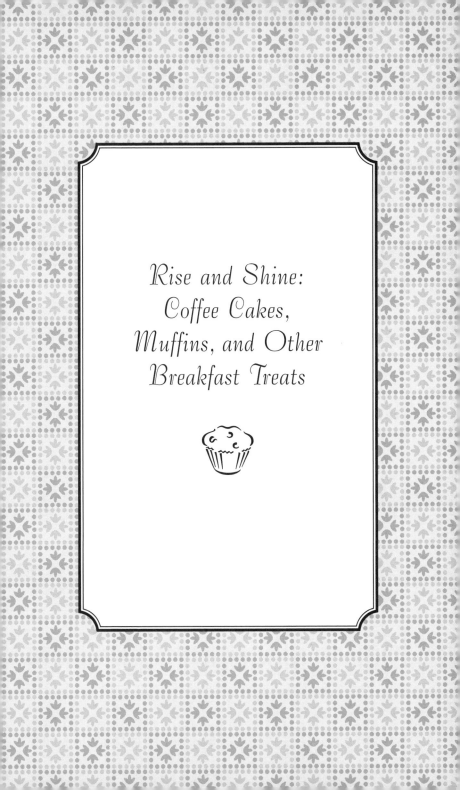

Cinnamon Swirl Coffee Cake

MAKES 9 SERVINGS

· ❋ ·

New Classic Method

This is quick enough to make for the family on the spur of the moment, and elegant enough for a company brunch. Its nutty flavor doesn't come from nuts themselves, but from nutlike cereal nuggets (Grape-Nuts), sprinkled on top to add fiber but hardly any fat. If your family loves spice as much as mine, double the topping mixture.

Nonstick canola oil spray

CAKE
> 1 $\frac{1}{2}$ cups whole wheat *pastry* flour (*spoon* into
>   measuring cup and level top)
> 1 $\frac{1}{2}$ teaspoons baking powder
> $\frac{1}{2}$ teaspoon baking soda
> $\frac{1}{8}$ teaspoon salt
>
> $\frac{3}{4}$ cup sugar
> $\frac{2}{3}$ cup 1 percent low-fat milk
> $\frac{1}{2}$ cup water
> 2 tablespoons canola oil
> 1 large egg

TOPPING
> 2 tablespoons unsweetened applesauce
> 2 teaspoons sugar
> 1 teaspoon ground cinnamon
> 2 tablespoons Grape-Nuts cereal

1. Position a rack in the center of the oven and preheat to 350° F. Lightly spray a nonstick 8-inch square baking pan with oil.

2. To make the cake, in a medium bowl, whisk the flour, baking powder, baking soda, and salt until well combined. Set aside.

3. In another medium bowl, using a handheld electric mixer set at high speed, beat the sugar, milk, water, oil, and egg until frothy, about 2 minutes. Make a well in the center of the dry ingredients and pour in the milk mixture. Using a spoon, stir just until combined (the batter will be a little lumpy, but that's okay). Do not overmix. Turn into the prepared pan.

4. To make the topping, in a small bowl, combine the applesauce, sugar, and cinnamon. Drop by heaping teaspoons onto the batter. Swirl a knife back and forth through the batter. Sprinkle the Grape-Nuts over the top.

5. Bake until the top of the cake springs back when gently touched in the center and the sides pull away from the pan, 30 to 35 minutes. Do not overbake. Cool in the pan on a wire cake rack for 10 minutes. Serve warm, or cool completely in the pan on a wire cake rack.

Nutritional Analysis

Each serving: *About 194 calories (8 percent from protein; 73 percent from carbohydrates; 19 percent from fat), 4 grams protein, 37 grams carbohydrates, 4 grams fat (less than 1 gram saturated fat), 24 milligrams cholesterol, 158 milligrams sodium*

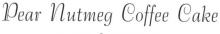

Pear Nutmeg Coffee Cake

· ✳ ·

New Classic Method

*H*ere's another old family recipe I have made over into a much healthier, equally tasty version. Freshly grated nutmeg really makes this cake. I have a small nutmeg grater, but the fine holes on a regular grater will do the job, too.

Nonstick canola oil spray

CAKE

1 cup plus 2 tablespoons whole wheat *pastry* flour
(*spoon* into measuring cup and level top to get
1 cup, then measure 2 level tablespoons)
³/₄ teaspoon baking soda
¹/₂ teaspoon ground cinnamon
¹/₂ teaspoon freshly grated nutmeg
¹/₈ teaspoon salt

1 large egg
¹/₂ cup sugar
¹/₃ cup plus 1 tablespoon unsweetened applesauce
¹/₃ cup plus 1 tablespoon low-fat buttermilk
1 ¹/₂ teaspoons canola oil
1 teaspoon vanilla extract
¹/₂ teaspoon almond extract (optional)

1 ripe Anjou pear, peeled, cored, and sliced into
¹/₂ -inch-thick wedges

TOPPING

2 tablespoons finely chopped walnuts
2 tablespoons sugar

1 tablespoon unsweetened applesauce

¼ teaspoon ground cinnamon

¼ teaspoon freshly grated nutmeg

1. Position a rack in the center of the oven and preheat to 350° F. Lightly spray a nonstick 8-inch round cake pan with oil.

2. To make the cake, whisk the flour, baking soda, cinnamon, nutmeg, and salt in a medium bowl to combine. Set aside.

3. In another medium bowl, using a handheld electric mixer set at high speed, beat the egg, sugar, applesauce, buttermilk, oil, vanilla, and almond extract until frothy, about 2 minutes. Make a well in the center of the dry ingredients and pour in the buttermilk mixture. Using a wooden spoon, stir just until combined. Do not overmix. Turn into the prepared pan. Using a gentle touch, smooth the top. Arrange the pears in a circle around the edges of the batter.

4. To make the topping, combine the walnuts, sugar, applesauce, cinnamon, and nutmeg in a small bowl. Drop teaspoons of the mixture over the top of the cake. Press the topping and pears gently into the batter.

5. Bake until the top of the cake springs back when gently touched in the center and the sides pull away from the pan, about 30 minutes. Do not overbake. Cool in the pan on a wire cake rack for 10 minutes. Serve warm, or cool completely in the pan on a wire cake rack.

Nutritional Analysis

Each serving: *About 157 calories (9 percent from protein; 76 percent from carbohydrates; 15 percent from fat), 4 grams protein, 31 grams carbohydrates, 3 grams fat (less than 1 gram saturated fat), 24 milligrams cholesterol, 117 milligrams sodium*

Sarah's Do-It-Your-Way Muffins

MAKES 12 MUFFINS

New Classic Method

I think every cook needs a basic healthy muffin recipe to whip up a batch whenever the mood strikes and with whatever goodies are around. When it's summertime, I'll stir in blueberries or raspberries. In autumn or winter, I'll add cranberries. Sometimes I'll mix in some pumpkin or prune puree instead of the applesauce, and these are especially good with raisins. In other words . . . do it your way!

Nonstick canola oil spray

2 cups unbleached all-purpose flour (*spoon* into measuring cup and level top)
1 ½ teaspoons baking powder
½ teaspoon baking soda
1 teaspoon ground cinnamon
½ teaspoon freshly grated nutmeg
⅛ teaspoon salt

¾ cup low-fat buttermilk
¾ cup unsweetened applesauce
⅔ cup packed dark brown sugar
1 large egg
1 ½ tablespoons canola oil
1 teaspoon vanilla extract

½ cup raisins

1. Position a rack in the center of the oven and preheat to 350° F. Lightly spray twelve 2 ¾ × 1 ½-inch nonstick muffin cups with oil.

2. In a medium bowl, whisk the flour, baking powder, baking soda, cinnamon, nutmeg, and salt until well combined. Set aside.

3. In another medium bowl, using a handheld electric mixer set at high speed, beat the buttermilk, applesauce, brown sugar, egg, oil, and vanilla until frothy, about 2 minutes. Make a well in the center of the dry ingredients and pour in the buttermilk mixture. Using a spoon, mix just until moistened (there should be a few traces of flour remaining). Gently fold in the raisins until the flour is incorporated. Do not overmix.

4. Divide the batter equally among the prepared muffin cups. Bake until the tops spring back when pressed gently in the center, about 20 minutes. Do not overbake. Cool in the pan on a wire cake rack for 10 minutes before removing from the cups. Serve warm or cool completely on the rack.

BERRY MUFFINS: Substitute ½ cup fresh or frozen (do not thaw) blueberries or raspberries for the raisins.

CHOCOLATE CHIP MUFFINS: Omit the raisins; add ¼ cup mini-chocolate chips.

CRANBERRY-PUMPKIN MUFFINS: Substitute ½ cup solid pack pumpkin for ½ cup of the applesauce and ½ cup fresh or frozen (do not thaw) cranberries for the raisins.

WINTER FRUIT MUFFINS: Substitute ½ cup prune baby food for ½ cup of the applesauce and ½ cup dried currants for the raisins.

NUT MUFFINS: Omit the raisins; sprinkle ¼ cup chopped walnuts or pecans over the tops of the muffins and press gently into the batter before baking.

Nutritional Analyses

Sarah's Muffins (each muffin): *About 176 calories (8 percent from protein; 79 percent from carbohydrates; 13 percent from fat), 3 grams protein, 35 grams carbohydrates, 3 grams fat (less than 1 gram saturated fat), 18 milligrams cholesterol, 124 milligrams sodium*

Berry Muffins (each muffin): *About 159 calories (8 percent from protein; 77 percent from carbohydrates; 14 percent from fat), 3 grams protein, 31 grams carbohydrates, 3 grams fat (less than 1 gram saturated fat), 18 milligrams cholesterol, 124 milligrams sodium*

Chocolate Chip Muffins (each muffin): *About 174 calories (8 percent from protein; 75 percent from carbohydrates; 17 percent from fat), 3 grams protein, 33 grams carbohydrates, 3 grams fat (less than 1 gram saturated fat), 18 milligrams cholesterol, 126 milligrams sodium*

Cranberry-Pumpkin Muffins (each muffin): *About 159 calories (8 percent from protein; 77 percent from carbohydrates; 14 percent from fat), 3 grams protein, 31 grams carbohydrates, 3 grams fat (less than 1 gram saturated fat), 18 milligrams cholesterol, 124 milligrams sodium*

Winter Fruit Muffins (each muffin): *About 175 calories (8 percent from protein; 79 percent from carbohydrates; 13 percent from fat), 3 grams protein, 34 grams carbohydrates, 3 grams fat (less than 1 gram saturated fat), 18 milligrams cholesterol, 123 milligrams sodium*

Nut Muffins (each muffin): *About 173 calories (9 percent from protein; 71 percent from carbohydrates; 20 percent from fat), 4 grams protein, 31 grams carbohydrates, 4 grams fat (less than 1 gram saturated fat), 18 milligrams cholesterol, 123 milligrams sodium*

Blueberry-Lemon Muffins

MAKES 12 MUFFINS

* ❋ *

New Class Method

Who can resist freshly baked blueberry muffins? In addition to their wonderful, summery flavor, they are loaded with vitamin C. These get an aromatic lift from fresh lemon. In the autumn, substitute fresh or frozen cranberries for the blueberries.

Nonstick canola oil spray

1 cup unbleached all-purpose flour *(spoon* into measuring cup and level top)
$^3/_4$ cup whole wheat flour (*spoon* into measuring cup and level top)
1 teaspoon ground cinnamon
1 teaspoon baking powder
$^1/_2$ teaspoon baking soda
$^1/_8$ teaspoon salt

1 cup unsweetened applesauce
$^1/_2$ cup sugar
1 large egg
2 tablespoons canola oil
Grated zest of 1 lemon or $^1/_4$ teaspoon pure lemon oil

1 cup fresh or frozen (do not thaw) blueberries

1. Position a rack in the center of the oven and preheat to 350° F. Lightly spray twelve $2^3/_4 \times 1^1/_2$-inch nonstick muffin cups with oil.

2. In a medium bowl, whisk the flours, cinnamon, baking powder, baking soda, and salt until well combined. Set aside.

3. In another medium bowl, using a handheld electric mixer set at

high speed, beat the applesauce, sugar, egg, oil, and lemon zest until frothy, about 2 minutes. Make a well in the center of the dry ingredients and pour in the applesauce mixture. Using a spoon, mix just until moistened (there should be a few traces of flour remaining). Gently fold in the berries until the flour is incorporated. Do not overmix.

4. Divide the batter equally among the prepared muffin cups. Bake until the tops spring back when pressed gently in the center, about 20 minutes. Do not overbake. Cool in the pan on a wire cake rack for 10 minutes before removing from the cups. Serve warm or cool completely on the rack.

Nutritional Analysis
Each muffin: *About 136 calories (8 percent from protein; 73 percent from carbohydrates; 19 percent from fat), 3 grams protein, 26 grams carbohydrates, 3 grams fat (less than 1 gram saturated fat), 18 milligrams cholesterol, 91 milligrams sodium*

Buttermilk Bran Muffins

· ✳ ·

New Classic Method

These bran muffins bake up moist and chewy. They're so good that my in-laws, Reed and Nancy, make a batch every couple of days for snacking. This is another recipe that shows how buttermilk works to tenderize and lighten many baked goods. Bran retains much of its natural oil and can quickly turn rancid, so always store it in the refrigerator or freezer. I like to use unprocessed sugar crystals (don't confuse this with brown sugar) to complement the bran's whole grain taste. Each muffin has over 2 grams of fiber.

Nonstick canola oil spray

1 cup unprocessed (miller's) wheat bran
²/₃ cup unbleached all-purpose flour (*spoon* into
    measuring cup and level top)
²/₃ cup whole wheat flour (*spoon* into measuring
    cup and level top)
1 ¼ teaspoons baking soda
⅛ teaspoon salt

1 ¼ cups low-fat buttermilk
½ cup raw sugar crystals (such as Sugar in
    the Raw) or granulated sugar
¼ cup unsweetened applesauce
1 large egg
1 ½ tablespoons canola oil
1 teaspoon vanilla extract

1. Position a rack in the center of the oven and preheat to 350° F. Lightly spray twelve 2 ¾ × 1 ½-inch nonstick muffin cups with oil.

34 · *The Healthy Oven Baking Book*

2. In a medium bowl, whisk the bran, flours, baking soda, and salt until well combined. Set aside.

3. In another medium bowl, using a handheld electric mixer set at high speed, beat the buttermilk, sugar, applesauce, egg, oil, and vanilla until frothy, about 2 minutes. Make a well in the center of the dry ingredients, and pour in the buttermilk mixture. Using a spoon, stir just until combined. Do not overmix.

4. Divide the batter equally among the prepared muffin cups. Bake until the tops spring back when pressed gently in the center, about 20 minutes. Do not overbake. Cool in the pan on a wire cake rack for 10 minutes before removing from the cups. Serve warm or cool completely on the rack.

RAISIN BRAN MUFFINS: Mix the batter just until moistened—there should be a few traces of flour remaining. Add ½ cup raisins and stir until combined. Do not overmix.

Nutritional Analyses

Buttermilk Bran Muffins (each muffin): *About 123 calories (11 percent from protein; 70 percent from carbohydrates; 19 percent from fat), 4 grams protein, 23 grams carbohydrates, 3 grams fat (less than 1 gram saturated fat), 19 milligrams cholesterol, 140 milligrams sodium*

Raisin Bran Muffins (each muffin): *About 141 calories (10 percent from protein; 73 percent from carbohydrates; 16 percent from fat), 4 grams protein, 28 grams carbohydrates, 3 grams fat (less than 1 gram saturated fat), 19 milligrams cholesterol, 141 milligrams sodium*

Cinnamon Streusel Muffins

MAKES 9 MUFFINS

· ✳ ·

New Classic Method

The kitchen will be filled with the heady aroma of cinnamon when you bake these wonderful muffins. There is no fruit in these to distract from their sugar-and-spice goodness.

Nonstick canola oil spray

STREUSEL
   2 tablespoons dark brown sugar
   1 tablespoon unbleached all-purpose flour
   1/4 teaspoon ground cinnamon

MUFFINS
   3/4 cup unbleached all-purpose flour (*spoon* into measuring cup and level top)
   3/4 cup whole wheat flour (*spoon* into measuring cup and level top)
   2 teaspoons ground cinnamon
   1 teaspoon baking powder
   1/2 teaspoon baking soda
   1/8 teaspoon salt

   1 cup unsweetened applesauce
   1/2 cup packed dark brown sugar
   1 large egg
   1 tablespoon canola oil
   1 teaspoon vanilla extract

1. Position a rack in the center of the oven and preheat to 350° F. Lightly spray nine 2 3/4 × 1 1/2-inch nonstick muffin cups with oil. (Fill the muffin cups you will not be using half-full with water, or the pan could smoke during baking.)

2. To make the streusel, mix the brown sugar, flour, and cinnamon until well combined. Set aside.

3. To make the muffins, in a medium bowl, whisk the flours, cinnamon, baking powder, baking soda, and salt until well combined. Set aside.

4. In another medium bowl, using a handheld electric mixer set at high speed, beat the applesauce, brown sugar, egg, oil, and vanilla until frothy, about 2 minutes. Make a well in the center of the dry ingredients and pour in the applesauce mixture. Stir with a spoon just until moistened. Do not overmix.

5. Spoon about 1 heaping tablespoon of the batter into each muffin cup. Sprinkle each with a scant teaspoon of the streusel. Top with the remaining batter, then with the remaining streusel.

6. Bake until the tops spring back when pressed gently in the center, about 20 minutes. Do not overbake. Cool in the pan on a wire cake rack for 10 minutes before removing from the cups. Serve warm or cool completely on the rack.

....

Nutritional Analysis
Each muffin: *About 169 calories (8 percent from protein; 80 percent from carbohydrates; 13 percent from fat), 3 grams protein, 34 grams carbohydrates, 2 grams fat (less than 1 gram saturated fat), 24 milligrams cholesterol, 125 milligrams sodium*

Raspberry Corn Muffins

MAKES 12 MUFFINS

· ❋ ·

New Classic Method

We have raspberry bushes in our backyard, and I was always looking for opportunities to use our seemingly endless harvest. It wasn't long before the raspberries found their way into our corn muffins, and now this is one of our favorite recipes. Please note the baking powder in this recipe is measured by a tablespoon.

Nonstick canola oil spray

1 ¼ cups yellow cornmeal, preferably stone-ground
¾ cup unbleached all-purpose flour (*spoon* into
    measuring cup and level top)
1 tablespoon baking powder
⅛ teaspoon salt

1 cup 1 percent low-fat milk
½ cup sugar
¼ cup unsweetened applesauce
1 large egg
1 tablespoon canola oil

½ cup fresh or frozen (do not thaw) raspberries

1. Position a rack in the center of the oven and preheat to 400° F. Lightly spray twelve 2 ¾ × 1 ½-inch nonstick muffin cups with oil.

2. In a medium bowl, whisk the cornmeal, flour, baking powder, and salt until well combined. Set aside.

3. In another medium bowl, using a handheld electric mixer set at high speed, beat the milk, sugar, applesauce, egg, and oil until frothy, about 2 minutes. Make a well in the center of the dry ingredients, and pour in the milk mixture. Using a spoon, stir just until moistened (there should be a few traces of flour remaining). Gently fold in the raspberries until the flour is incorporated. The batter will be thin. Do not overmix.

4. Divide the batter equally among the prepared muffin cups. Bake until the tops spring back when pressed gently in the center, 15 to 20 minutes. Do not overbake. Cool in the pan on a wire cake rack for 10 minutes before removing from the cups. Serve warm or cool completely on the rack.

Nutritional Analysis
Each muffin: *About 141 calories (9 percent from protein; 78 percent from carbohydrates; 13 percent from fat), 3 grams protein, 28 grams carbohydrates, 2 grams fat (less than 1 gram saturated fat), 19 milligrams cholesterol, 121 milligrams sodium*

Oatmeal Maple Muffins

MAKES 12 MUFFINS

· ✳ ·

New Class Method

Apples, raisins, oatmeal, maple syrup—what wonderful flavors to wake up to! If I know I am going to make muffins for breakfast, sometimes I'll prepare the ingredients the night before as a timesaver. Just whisk the dry ingredients in their bowl, cover, and let stand at room temperature. Combine the liquid ingredients, cover, and refrigerate. When ready to bake, just whip up the liquid ingredients with the electric mixer and proceed.

Nonstick canola oil spray

1 ½ cups unbleached all-purpose flour (*spoon* into measuring cup and level top)
¾ cup quick-cooking oatmeal (see Note)
1 ½ teaspoons baking powder
1 teaspoon ground cinnamon
½ teaspoon baking soda
⅛ teaspoon salt

¾ cup unsweetened applesauce
½ cup pure maple syrup, preferably Grade B
1 large egg
1 ½ tablespoons canola oil
1 teaspoon vanilla extract

½ cup peeled, shredded Granny Smith apple

½ cup raisins

1. Position a rack in the center of the oven and preheat to 350° F. Lightly spray twelve 2 ¾ × 1 ½-inch nonstick muffin cups with oil.

2. In a medium bowl, whisk the flour, oatmeal, baking powder, cinnamon, baking soda, and salt until well combined. Set aside.

3. In another medium bowl, using a handheld electric mixer set at high speed, beat the applesauce, maple syrup, egg, oil, and vanilla until frothy, about 2 minutes. Make a well in the center of the dry ingredients, and pour in the applesauce mixture. Using a spoon, stir just until moistened (there should be a few traces of flour remaining). Gently fold in the shredded apple and the raisins until the flour is incorporated. Do not overmix.

4. Divide the batter equally among the prepared muffin cups. Bake until the tops spring back when pressed gently in the center, about 20 minutes. Do not overbake. Let cool in the pan on a wire cake rack for 10 minutes before removing from the cups. Serve warm or cool completely on the rack.

N o t e : If you have the time, lightly toast the oats in a 350° F oven, stirring often, until golden around the edges, about 7 minutes. Cool the oats completely before using

Nutritional Analysis
Each muffin: *About 164 calories (8 percent from protein; 78 percent from carbohydrates; 14 percent from fat), 3 grams protein, 33 grams carbohydrates, 3 grams fat (less than 1 gram saturated fat), 18 milligrams cholesterol, 118 milligrams sodium*

Pumpkin-Ginger Muffins

MAKES 12 MUFFINS

· ❊ ·

New Classic Method

*P*umpkin is full of beta-carotene and vitamin A, so these muffins are especially healthful as well as deliciously spicy. There's more than one way to get ginger's zip into these muffins. I like to use 2 teaspoons grated fresh ginger, but you can substitute an equal amount of minced crystallized ginger or 1 teaspoon of ground ginger. These are a great breakfast treat, served plain with a bracing cup of coffee or tea. But if you want to gild the lily, frost them with Orange Cream Cheese Frosting (page 134) and garnish with a sprinkling of chopped pumpkin seeds or pecans.

Nonstick canola oil spray

2 $^1/_2$ cups whole wheat flour (*spoon* into
    measuring cup and level top)
1 $^1/_2$ teaspoons baking soda
1 teaspoon ground cinnamon
$^1/_8$ teaspoon salt

1 cup packed dark brown sugar
$^3/_4$ cup canned pumpkin
$^3/_4$ cup plain nonfat yogurt
1 large egg
1 tablespoon canola oil
2 teaspoons grated fresh ginger (use the
    small holes on a box grater)

1. Position a rack in the center of the oven and preheat to 350° F. Lightly spray twelve 2 $^3/_4$ × 1 $^1/_2$-inch nonstick muffin cups with nonstick spray.

2. In a medium bowl, whisk the flour, baking soda, cinnamon, and salt until well combined. Set aside.

3. In another medium bowl, using a handheld electric mixer set at high speed, beat the brown sugar, pumpkin, yogurt, egg, oil, and ginger until frothy, about 2 minutes. Make a well in the center of the dry ingredients, and pour in the pumpkin mixture. Using a spoon, stir just until combined. Do not overmix.

4. Divide the batter equally among the prepared muffin cups. Bake until the tops spring back when pressed gently in the center, about 20 minutes. Do not overbake. Cool in the pan on a wire cake rack for 10 minutes before removing from the cups. Serve warm or completely cool on the rack at room temperature.

Nutritional Analysis
Each muffin: *About 183 calories (10 percent from protein; 80 percent from carbohydrates; 10 percent from fat), 5 grams protein, 38 grams carbohydrates, 2 grams fat (less than 1 gram saturated fat), 18 milligrams cholesterol, 149 milligrams sodium*

Baked Whole Wheat Doughnuts

MAKES 6 DOUGHNUTS

· ✸ ·

New Classic Method

When my friend Mäni Niall owned Mäni's Bakery in Los Angeles, a movie company came to him to develop a healthful doughnut to use as a prop in a Danny DeVito movie (Danny is a very health-conscious eater, and didn't want to eat junk, even in the name of art). Mäni's solution, a baked doughnut, took L.A. by storm. These are a little different from his, as Mäni cooks with fruit juices instead of sugar, but mine are just as good. You'll need mini-fluted tube pans for these.

Nonstick canola oil spray

DOUGHNUTS

1 cup plus 2 tablespoons whole wheat *pastry* flour
(*spoon* into measuring cup and level top to get 1 cup,
then measure 2 level tablespoons)
¾ teaspoon baking soda
½ teaspoon ground cinnamon
⅛ teaspoon salt

½ cup sugar
⅓ cup plus 1 tablespoon unsweetened applesauce
⅓ cup plus 1 tablespoon low-fat buttermilk
1 large egg
1 ½ teaspoons canola oil
1 teaspoon vanilla extract

GLAZE

1 cup confectioners' sugar
2 tablespoons apple juice or water
1 teaspoon vanilla extract

1. Position a rack in the center of the oven and preheat to 350° F. Generously spray six 4-inch nonstick mini-fluted tube (Bundtlette) pans (Nordic Ware) with oil.

2. To make the doughnuts, in a medium bowl, whisk the flour, baking soda, cinnamon, and salt until well combined. Set aside.

3. In another medium bowl, using a handheld electric mixer set at high speed, beat the granulated sugar, applesauce, buttermilk, egg, oil, and vanilla until frothy, about 2 minutes. Make a well in the center of the dry ingredients, and pour in the applesauce mixture. Using a spoon, stir just until combined. Do not overmix.

4. Divide the batter equally among the prepared molds. Bake until the tops spring back when pressed gently around the edges, 15 to 20 minutes. Do not overbake. Cool in the molds on a wire cake rack for 5 minutes. Then, run a knife around the inside of the molds to release the doughnuts. Invert onto the rack and cool completely.

5. To make the glaze, whisk the confectioners' sugar, apple juice, and vanilla until smooth. Drizzle over the tops of the doughnuts. Let stand until the glaze is set, about 30 minutes.

....

Nutritional Analysis

Each doughnut: *About 250 calories (7 percent from protein; 84 percent from carbohydrates; 9 percent from fat), 5 grams protein, 54 grams carbohydrates, 3 grams fat (less than 1 gram saturated fat), 36 milligrams cholesterol, 175 milligrams sodium*

Lemon Tea Scones

MAKES 12 SCONES

· ✳ ·

New Classic Method

These tender scones are lovely with a cup of hot tea, especially with a slathering of raspberry fruit spread. If you live in California, you will probably be able to make these with Meyer lemons. Small, thin-skinned, and packed with flavor, they are rarely available in stores, but many people grow them in their backyards—just the way my family did when we lived in Los Angeles.

2 cups whole wheat *pastry* flour (*spoon* into
    measuring cup and level top)
1 ½ teaspoons baking powder
1 teaspoon baking soda
⅛ teaspoon salt

1 cup low-fat buttermilk
¼ cup sugar
1 large egg
1 tablespoon canola oil
Grated zest of 2 lemons or a generous
    ¼ teaspoon pure lemon oil

Confectioners' sugar for sprinkling

1. Position a rack in the center of the oven and preheat to 350° F. Lightly spray a nonstick baking sheet with oil.

2. In a medium bowl, whisk the flour, baking powder, baking soda, and salt until well combined. Set aside.

3. In another medium bowl, using a handheld electric mixer set at high speed, beat the buttermilk, sugar, egg, oil, and lemon zest until lightened and frothy, about 2 minutes. Make a well in the center of the dry ingredients and pour in the buttermilk mixture. Using a spoon, stir just until combined. Do not overmix.

4. Drop $1/4$ cupfuls of the dough onto a prepared baking sheet spacing them about 2 inches apart. Bake until the tops are golden brown and tops spring back when lightly pressed in the center, 15 to 20 minutes. Do not overbake. Remove from the pan with a metal spatula and cool for 5 to 10 minutes on a wire cake rack. Serve warm.

ORANGE CARAWAY SCONES: Not too sweet, these are delicious served with dinner. Add 1 tablespoon caraway seed to the dry ingredients. Substitute the grated zest of 1 orange or $1/4$ teaspoon pure orange oil for the lemon zest.

....

Nutritional Analyses
Lemon Tea Scones (each scone): *About 116 calories (13 percent from protein; 71 percent from carbohydrates; 16 percent from fat), 4 grams protein, 21 grams carbohydrates, 2 grams fat (less than 1 gram saturated fat), 19 milligrams cholesterol, 159 milligrams sodium*
Orange Caraway Scones (each scone): *About 117 calories (13 percent from protein; 71 percent from carbohydrates; 16 percent from fat), 4 grams protein, 22 grams carbohydrates, 2 grams fat (less than 1 gram saturated fat), 19 milligrams cholesterol, 159 milligrams sodium*

Good Morning Buttermilk Pancakes

MAKES 9 PANCAKES

· ❋ ·

New Classic Method

*M*aking pancakes for the whole family is one of the nicest ways to start the day. (Whenever I have a straggling kid who can't get out of bed, the aroma of pancakes cooking on the griddle rouses him or her in no time.) Hotcakes are simple to make, and I have so many variations I can hardly decide which one to make. I hope these pancakes become a weekend event at your house, too. Serve them with pure maple syrup.

Nonstick canola oil spray

1 cup unbleached all-purpose flour (*spoon* into measuring cup and level top)
$\frac{1}{2}$ teaspoon baking soda
Pinch of salt

1 $\frac{1}{4}$ cups low-fat buttermilk
1 large egg
2 tablespoons sugar
1 tablespoon canola oil

1. Preheat a griddle or large skillet over medium-high heat until a splash of water sprinkled on the surface turns into tiny droplets.
2. Meanwhile, in a medium bowl, whisk the flour, baking soda, and salt until well combined.
3. In another medium bowl, whisk the buttermilk, egg, sugar, and oil, until combined. Make a well in the center of the dry ingredients and pour in the buttermilk mixture. Using a spoon, stir just until combined. The batter will be thick. Do not overmix.
4. Spray the griddle lightly with oil spray. For each pancake, pour $\frac{1}{4}$ cup of the batter onto the hot griddle. Cook until tiny bubbles appear on

the top and the edges look cooked. Turn with a pancake turner and continue cooking until the underside is browned. Spray the griddle in between batches. Serve hot, with maple syrup.

WHOLE WHEAT–ORANGE PANCAKES: Substitute $^1/_2$ cup whole wheat flour and $^1/_2$ cup unbleached flour for the 1 cup flour. Add the grated zest of $^1/_2$ orange or $^1/_4$ teaspoon pure orange oil and a few gratings of nutmeg to the buttermilk mixture.

BLUEBERRY PANCAKES: Sprinkle 1 tablespoon fresh or frozen (do not thaw) blueberries on top of each pancake right after it is poured onto the griddle. If desired, add the grated zest of 1 lemon or $^1/_4$ teaspoon pure lemon oil to the buttermilk mixture.

PUMPKIN PANCAKES: Add $^1/_2$ teaspoon ground cinnamon, $^1/_4$ teaspoon ground ginger, and $^1/_8$ teaspoon ground cloves to the dry ingredients. Add $^1/_2$ cup canned pumpkin to the buttermilk mixture. For a deeper ginger flavor, mix the batter just until moistened, add 1 tablespoon minced crystallized ginger, and continue mixing just until combined.

....

Nutritional Analyses

Buttermilk Pancakes (each pancake): *About 96 calories (14 percent from protein; 63 percent from carbohydrates; 24 percent from fat), 3 grams protein, 15 grams carbohydrates, 3 grams fat (less than 1 gram saturated fat), 25 milligrams cholesterol, 112 milligrams sodium*

Whole Wheat–Orange Pancakes (each pancake): *About 93 calories (14 percent from protein; 61 percent from carbohydrates; 24 percent from fat), 3 grams protein, 15 grams carbohydrates, 3 grams fat (less than 1 gram saturated fat), 25 milligrams cholesterol, 112 milligrams sodium*

Blueberry Pancakes (each pancake): *About 101 calories (13 percent from protein; 64 percent from carbohydrates; 23 percent from fat), 3 grams protein, 16 grams carbohydrates, 3 grams fat (less than 1 gram saturated fat), 25 milligrams cholesterol, 113 milligrams sodium*

Pumpkin Pancakes (each pancake): *About 108 calories (13 percent from protein; 66 percent from carbohydrates; 21 percent from fat), 3 grams protein, 18 grams carbohydrates, 3 grams fat (less than 1 gram saturated fat), 25 milligrams cholesterol, 113 milligrams sodium*

Baked French Toast with Raspberry Syrup

MAKES 8 SERVINGS

· ✻ ·

*T*here's no need to fry French toast—baked is just as good, if not better! Of course, you could serve these with plain maple syrup, but
this easy raspberry version is scrumptious.

> **Nonstick canola oil spray**
>
> **RASPBERRY SYRUP**
> 1 ½ **cups fresh or frozen (do not thaw) raspberries**
> ¾ **cup pure maple syrup, preferably grade B**
>
> **FRENCH TOAST**
> **One 12-ounce can evaporated skimmed milk**
> **1 large egg**
> ¼ **cup packed dark brown sugar**
> **2 large egg whites**
> **1 teaspoon vanilla extract**
> **16 slices day-old French baguette or Italian bread,**
> **cut ½ inch thick**
> **Confectioners' sugar and ground cinnamon for**
> **sprinkling**
> **Fresh raspberries, for garnish**

1. Position a rack in the center of the oven and preheat to 400° F.
Lightly spray a nonstick baking sheet with oil.

2. To make the syrup, puree the raspberries and maple syrup together in a blender or food processor. Pour into a small saucepan. Stirring often, bring to a simmer over medium-low heat. If desired, rub
through a wire strainer to remove the seeds. Keep warm.

3. In a large bowl, whisk the evaporated milk, egg, brown sugar, egg whites, and vanilla until combined. One at a time, briefly dip the bread slices into the milk mixture and place on the prepared baking sheet.

4. Bake for about 10 minutes until golden brown. Turn, and continue to bake until golden brown for approximately 10 minutes more. Serve hot, sprinkled with the confectioners' sugar and cinnamon and garnished with the raspberries. Pass the raspberry syrup on the side.

Nutritional Analysis

Each serving (2 slices with syrup): *About 368 calories (13 percent from protein; 78 percent from carbohydrates; 9 percent from fat), 12 grams protein, 73 grams carbohydrates, 4 grams fat (less than 1 gram saturated fat), 29 milligrams cholesterol, 495 milligrams sodium*

Whole Grain Waffles

MAKES ABOUT 8 WAFFLES

· ✻ ·

New Classic Method

*K*ids love waffles—I'll bet the magic of seeing the waffle batter rising up between the waffle grids has as much to do with their popularity as their taste. Be sure to use a nonstick waffle iron. Serve with pure maple syrup or the raspberry syrup on page 50.

³/₄ cup unbleached all-purpose flour (*spoon* into
   measuring cup and level top)
³/₄ cup whole wheat *pastry* flour or whole wheat
   flour (*spoon* into measuring cup and level top)
¹/₄ cup unprocessed (miller's) wheat bran
2 teaspoons baking powder
¹/₈ teaspoon salt

1 ¹/₄ cups 1 percent low-fat milk
¹/₄ cup canola oil
1 large egg
2 large egg whites
2 tablespoons sugar

Nonstick canola oil spray

1. Position a rack in the center of the oven and preheat to 200° F. Preheat a nonstick waffle iron according to the manufacturer's directions.

2. In a medium bowl, whisk the flours, bran, baking powder, and salt, until well combined. Set aside.

3. In another medium bowl, whisk the milk, oil, egg, egg whites, and sugar. Make a well in the center of the dry ingredients and pour in the milk mixture. Using a spoon, stir just until combined. Do not overmix.

4. Generously spray both sides of the waffle iron with oil. Pour enough batter into the center of the lower iron to come within 1 inch of the edges. Cover and cook as the manufacturer directs, until the waffle batter stops steaming, 2 to 3 minutes, depending on the heat of the iron. Do not lift the cover while cooking. Transfer to a baking sheet and keep warm in the oven while cooking the remaining waffles. Between batches, spray both sides of the waffle iron with oil. Serve hot, with the maple syrup.

ORANGE-PECAN WAFFLES: Add the grated zest of 1 orange or ¼ teaspoon pure orange oil to the liquid ingredients. Pour into the dry ingredients and stir just until moistened. Add ¼ cup finely chopped pecans, and fold until the batter is combined.

BUTTERMILK WAFFLES: Omit the whole wheat pastry flour. Increase the unbleached flour to 1½ cups. Omit baking powder and add in ¾ teaspoon baking soda. Substitute low-fat buttermilk for the 1 percent low-fat milk.

....

Nutritional Analyses

Whole Grain Waffles (each waffle): *About 187 calories (12 percent from protein; 49 percent from carbohydrates; 39 percent from fat), 6 grams protein, 24 grams carbohydrates, 8 grams fat (less than 1 gram saturated fat), 28 milligrams cholesterol, 157 milligrams sodium*

Orange-Pecan Waffles (each waffle): *About 211 calories (11 percent calories from protein; 45 percent from carbohydrates; 43 percent from fat), 6 grams protein, 25 grams carbohydrates, 11 grams fat (less than 1 gram saturated fat), 28 milligrams cholesterol, 157 milligrams sodium*

Buttermilk Waffles (each waffle): *About 192 calories (12 percent calories from protein; 51 percent from carbohydrates; 38 percent from fat), 6 grams protein, 24 grams carbohydrates, 8 grams fat (less than 1 gram saturated fat), 28 milligrams cholesterol, 173 milligrams sodium*

In a Flash: Quick Breads and Cakes

Applesauce-Raisin Snackin' Cake

· ❈ ·

New Classic Method

Often I need to whip up a snack, lunch-box treat, or easy family dessert—fast. That's where this recipe comes in. It can be made in minutes with ingredients any healthful cook always has on hand, and flavored with whatever strikes your fancy—raisins, dried fruits (cranberries, blueberries, apples, cherries), nuts, or chocolate chips. The batter can be baked in a 6-cup fluted tube cake pan for a decorative shape.

Nonstick canola oil spray

1 $\frac{1}{4}$ cups whole wheat *pastry* flour (*spoon* into
    measuring cup and level top)
$\frac{3}{4}$ teaspoon baking soda
$\frac{1}{2}$ teaspoon ground cinnamon
$\frac{1}{8}$ teaspoon nutmeg
Pinch of salt

$\frac{1}{2}$ cup packed dark brown sugar
$\frac{1}{3}$ cup plus 1 tablespoon low-fat buttermilk
$\frac{1}{3}$ cup plus 1 tablespoon unsweetened applesauce
1 large egg
1 $\frac{1}{2}$ teaspoons canola oil
1 teaspoon vanilla extract

$\frac{1}{2}$ cup raisins

1. Position a rack in the center of the oven and preheat to 350° F. Lightly spray an 8-inch square nonstick baking pan (or generously spray a 6-cup nonstick fluted tube cake pan) with oil.

2. In a medium bowl, whisk the flour, baking soda, cinnamon, nutmeg, and salt until well combined. Set aside.

3. In another medium bowl, using a handheld electric mixer set at high speed, beat the brown sugar, buttermilk, applesauce, egg, oil, and vanilla until light in color and frothy, about 2 minutes. Make a well in the center of the dry ingredients and pour in the buttermilk mixture. Using a spoon, stir just until moistened (there should be few wisps of flour remaining). Add the raisins and stir just until the batter is smooth. Do not overmix. Using a gentle touch, spread the batter evenly in the prepared pan.

4. Bake until the top of the cake springs back when touched gently in the center and the edges are golden brown, 15 to 20 minutes (25 to 30 minutes for a fluted tube pan). Do not overbake. Cool in the pan on a wire cake rack for 10 minutes. Invert onto the rack and cool completely.

Nutritional Analysis
Each serving: *About 157 calories (9 percent from protein; 82 percent from carbohydrates; 10 percent from fat), 4 grams protein, 33 grams carbohydrates, 2 grams fat (less than 1 gram saturated fat), 24 milligrams cholesterol, 115 milligrams sodium*

Apricot Corn Cake

MAKES 8 SERVINGS

· ❋ ·

New Classic Method

I love to make this cake with apricot-mango yogurt, but it can be enhanced with other flavors such as peach or blueberry. Or, use 8 ounces of plain nonfat yogurt with 3 tablespoons of your favorite all-fruit spread.

Nonstick canola oil spray

1 cup yellow cornmeal, preferably stone-ground
1 cup unbleached all-purpose flour (*spoon* into
    measuring cup and level top)
1 teaspoon baking soda
1/8 teaspoon salt

One 8-ounce container fruit-flavored nonfat yogurt,
    preferably apricot-mango
1/2 cup packed dark brown sugar
1 large egg
2 teaspoons canola oil
1 teaspoon vanilla extract

1. Position a rack in the center of the oven and preheat to 350° F. Lightly spray an 8-inch square nonstick cake pan with oil.
2. In a medium bowl, whisk the cornmeal, flour, baking soda, and salt until well combined. Set aside.
3. In another medium bowl, using a handheld electric mixer set at high speed, beat the yogurt, brown sugar, egg, oil, and vanilla until frothy, about 2 minutes. Make a well in the center of the dry ingredients and pour in the yogurt mixture. Using a spoon, stir just until combined.

Do not overmix. Turn into the prepared pan. Using a gentle touch, smooth the top.

4. Bake until the cake is golden brown and the top springs back when pressed in the center, about 30 minutes. Do not overbake. Cool in the pan on a wire cake rack for 10 minutes. Serve warm or cool completely in the pan on a wire rack.

Nutritional Analysis

Each serving: *About 217 calories (9 percent from protein; 82 percent from carbohydrates; 9 percent from fat), 5 grams protein, 44 grams carbohydrates, 2 grams fat (less than 1 gram saturated fat), 27 milligrams cholesterol, 165 milligrams sodium*

New-Fashioned Banana Loaf

· 🌟 ·

New Classic Method

One of my Healthy Oven customers, Susan in San Diego, sent me her banana bread recipe for a reduced-fat makeover. Her original recipe had 1 cup of butter, which has about 1,798 calories, 192 fat grams, and 528 milligrams of cholesterol. Now we can all enjoy this American classic with a clear conscience. Banana bread (especially this low-fat version) is a prime candidate for add-ins, like 1/2 cup fresh blueberries or 1/3 cup mini-chocolate chips.

Nonstick canola oil spray

1 cup unbleached all-purpose flour (*spoon* into
   measuring cup and level top)
1 cup whole wheat flour (*spoon* into measuring cup and
   level top)
1 teaspoon baking soda
1 teaspoon ground cinnamon
1/4 teaspoon freshly grated nutmeg
1/8 teaspoon salt

1 cup packed dark brown sugar
1 cup mashed ripe bananas (about 2 large bananas)
3/4 cup unsweetened applesauce
1/2 cup low-fat buttermilk
1 large egg
1 tablespoon canola oil
1 teaspoon vanilla extract

1. Position a rack in the center of the oven and preheat to 350° F. Line the bottom of a 9 × 5 × 3-inch nonstick loaf pan with waxed paper and lightly spray the inside of the pan with oil.

2. In a medium bowl, whisk the flours, baking soda, cinnamon, nutmeg, and salt until well combined. Set aside.

3. In another medium bowl, using a handheld electric mixer set at high speed, beat the brown sugar, mashed bananas, applesauce, buttermilk, egg, oil, and vanilla until lightened and frothy, about 2 minutes. Make a well in the center of the dry ingredients and pour in the banana mixture. Using a spoon, stir just until combined. Do not overmix. Using a gentle touch, spread in the prepared pan.

4. Bake until cracks appear on the top, the loaf springs back when pressed gently in the center, and the sides are beginning to pull away from the pan, 55 to 60 minutes. Do not overbake. Cool in the pan on a wire cake rack for 10 minutes. Unmold onto the rack and peel off the paper. Turn right side up and cool completely.

Nutritional Analysis

Each serving: *About 186 calories (7 percent from protein; 83 percent from carbohydrates; 10 percent from fat), 4 grams protein, 40 grams carbohydrates, 2 grams fat (less than 1 gram saturated fat), 18 milligrams cholesterol, 113 milligrams sodium*

Carrot and Orange Tea Loaf

MAKES 12 SERVINGS

· 🎇 ·

New Class Method

When I was in college, I participated in the Student Garden Project, growing ecological organic produce. Therefore, I was never at a loss for vegetables, just for enough recipes to use them in. Carrot cake became a favorite with just about anyone who went to college in the seventies, but the original version used 1 cup of vegetable oil (about 208 fat grams right there!) Here's my updated, healthier loaf—still brimming with wholesome flavor. Use organic carrots for the best, sweetest, taste.

Nonstick canola oil spray

1 cup unbleached all-purpose flour (*spoon* into
   measuring cup and level top)
1 cup whole wheat flour (*spoon* into measuring
   cup and level top)
1 teaspoon baking soda
1/8 teaspoon salt

1 cup sugar
3/4 cup unsweetened applesauce
1/2 cup low-fat buttermilk
1 large egg
2 large egg whites
1 tablespoon canola oil
Grated zest of 1 orange or 1/4 teaspoon pure orange oil

1 cup shredded carrots, preferably organic

1/2 cup raisins

1. Position a rack in the center of the oven and preheat to 350° F. Line the bottom of a 9 × 5 × 3-inch nonstick loaf pan with waxed paper and lightly spray the inside of the pan with oil.

2. In a medium bowl, whisk the flours, baking soda, and salt until well combined. Set aside.

3. In another medium bowl, using a handheld electric mixer set at high speed, beat the sugar, applesauce, buttermilk, egg, egg whites, oil, and orange zest until frothy, about 2 minutes. Make a well in the center of the dry ingredients and pour in the buttermilk mixture. Using a spoon, stir just until moistened (there should be wisps of flour remaining). Add the carrots and raisins and stir just until smooth. Do not overmix. Using a gentle touch, spread in the prepared pan.

4. Bake until the top of the loaf springs back when pressed gently in the center, and the sides are beginning to pull away from the pan, about 1 hour. Do not overbake. Cool in the pan on a wire cake rack for 10 minutes. Unmold onto the rack and peel off the waxed paper. Turn right side up and cool completely.

Nutritional Analysis
Each serving: *About 184 calories (9 percent from protein; 82 percent from carbohydrates; 9 percent from fat), 4 grams protein, 40 grams carbohydrates, 2 grams fat (less than 1 gram saturated fat), 18 milligrams cholesterol, 121 milligrams sodium*

Chocolate Fudge Muffins

MAKES 12 MUFFINS

· ※ ·

New Classic Method

*A*re they muffins, or are they cupcakes? These are just a bit too sweet for the breakfast table, but many a muffin is enjoyed as an afternoon snack, too. They're the chocolatiest muffins around. Grown-ups love them with their coffee or tea, and kids devour them with a glass of milk. With a little frosting spread on top, I've served them to the kids as party cupcakes, too.

Nonstick canola oil spray

1 ½ cups unbleached all-purpose flour (*spoon* into
    measuring cup and level top)
½ cup Dutch-process cocoa powder (*spoon* into
    measuring cup and level top)
1 ½ teaspoons baking powder
½ teaspoon baking soda
⅛ teaspoon salt

1 ounce bittersweet or semisweet chocolate
¾ cup sugar
1 cup unsweetened applesauce
½ cup low-fat buttermilk
1 large egg
1 tablespoon unsalted butter, melted
2 teaspoons vanilla extract
1 teaspoon instant espresso powder

Fudgy Chocolate Frosting (page 133)

1. Position a rack in the center of the oven and preheat to 350° F. Lightly spray twelve 2 ¾ × 1 ½-inch nonstick muffin cups with oil.

2. In a medium bowl, whisk the flour, cocoa, baking powder, baking soda, and salt until well combined. Set aside.

3. Melt the chocolate according to the instructions on pages 256 to 257. Let the chocolate cool until tepid, but still liquid. In a medium bowl, using a handheld electric mixer set at high speed, beat the melted chocolate with the sugar, applesauce, buttermilk, egg, melted butter, vanilla, and espresso powder until frothy, about 2 minutes. Make a well in the center of the dry ingredients and pour in the applesauce mixture. Using a spoon, stir just until combined. Do not overmix.

4. Divide the batter equally among the prepared muffin cups. Bake until the tops feel firm when pressed in the center, 20 to 25 minutes. Do not overbake. Cool in the pan on a wire cake rack for 10 minutes before removing from the cups. Cool completely on the wire cake rack, then, if desired, frost the muffins (page 133).

Nutritional Analyses

Each muffin (unfrosted): *About 151 calories (8 percent from protein; 78 percent from carbohydrates; 14 percent from fat), 3 grams protein, 31 grams carbohydrates, 2 grams fat (less than 1 gram saturated fat), 21 milligrams cholesterol, 118 milligrams sodium*

Each muffin (with frosting): *About 222 calories (6 percent from protein; 75 percent from carbohydrates; 18 percent from fat), 4 grams protein, 45 grams carbohydrates, 5 grams fat (2 grams saturated fat), 23 milligrams cholesterol, 120 milligrams sodium*

Chocolate Chip and Espresso Cake

MAKES 9 SERVINGS

· ❋ ·

New Classic Method

When the kids are around, I make this with chocolate chips. Adults who love coffee may prefer finely chopped chocolate-covered espresso beans, found at specialty food stores. Either way, its a fudgy, chocolatey cake that always gets applause.

Nonstick canola oil spray

1 cup whole wheat *pastry* flour (*spoon* into measuring cup and level top)

$^1/_2$ cup Dutch-process cocoa powder (*spoon* into measuring cup and level top)

$^1/_2$ teaspoon baking powder

$^1/_2$ teaspoon baking soda

$^1/_8$ teaspoon salt

$^3/_4$ cup packed dark brown sugar

$^1/_2$ cup unsweetened applesauce

$^1/_3$ cup 1 percent low-fat milk

$^1/_4$ cup instant nonfat dry milk powder (do not reconstitute)

1 teaspoon instant espresso powder

1 large egg

1 teaspoon vanilla extract

$^1/_3$ cup semisweet mini-chocolate chips

1. Position a rack in the center of the oven and preheat to 350° F. Lightly spray an 8-inch square nonstick baking dish with oil.

2. Whisk the flour, cocoa, baking powder, baking soda, and salt in a medium bowl. Set aside.

3. In another medium bowl, using a handheld electric mixer set at high speed, beat the brown sugar, applesauce, instant dry milk powder, espresso powder, egg, and vanilla until frothy, about 2 minutes. Make a well in the center of the dry ingredients and pour in the milk mixture. Using a spoon, stir just until moistened (there should be wisps of flour remaining). Add the chocolate chips and stir just until the flour is incorporated. Do not overmix. Using a gentle touch, spread the batter in the prepared pan.

4. Bake until the sides of the cake are beginning to pull away from the pan, about 25 minutes. (The center of the cake may seem underdone.) Do not overbake. Cool in the pan on a wire cake rack for 10 minutes. Invert onto the rack and cool completely.

....

Nutritional Analysis
Each serving: *About 183 calories (9 percent from protein; 76 percent from carbohydrates; 14 percent from fat), 5 grams protein, 38 grams carbohydrates, 3 grams fat (less than 1 gram saturated fat), 24 milligrams cholesterol, 213 milligrams sodium*

Herbed Corn Bread Squares

MAKES 9 SERVINGS

· ✻ ·

New Classic Method

Warm corn bread, scented with thyme and sage, is a fine supper side dish. When I lived in Arizona, I learned to make corn bread with blue cornmeal, which can be found at some natural food stores. Blue cornmeal has an even richer corn flavor than the familiar yellow version, and blueberries accent the color.

Nonstick canola oil spray

1 cup yellow cornmeal, preferably stone-ground
 (see variation)

1 cup unbleached all-purpose flour (*spoon* into
 measuring cup and level top)

1 tablespoon chopped fresh thyme or 1 teaspoon
 dried 1 ½ teaspoons chopped fresh sage or
 ½ teaspoon dried

2 teaspoons baking powder

½ teaspoon baking soda

⅛ teaspoon salt

1 cup unsweetened applesauce

½ cup 1 percent low-fat milk

⅓ cup sugar

1 large egg

2 tablespoons unsalted butter, melted and
 slightly cooled

1. Position a rack in the center of the oven and preheat to 425° F. Lightly spray an 8-inch square nonstick baking pan with oil.

2. In a medium bowl, whisk the cornmeal, flour, thyme, sage, baking powder, baking soda, and salt until well combined. Set aside.

3. In another medium bowl, using a handheld electric mixer set at high speed, beat the applesauce, milk, sugar, and egg until frothy, about 2 minutes. Make a well in the center of the dry ingredients and pour in the applesauce mixture. Using a spoon, stir just until moistened (there should be a few wisps of flour remaining). Gently fold in the melted butter until the flour is incorporated. Do not overmix. Turn into the prepared baking pan.

4. Bake until the top is golden brown and springs back when pressed in the center, 20 to 25 minutes. Do not overbake. Cool in the pan on a wire cake rack for 10 minutes. Serve warm, or cool completely.

BLUE CORN BREAD WITH BLUEBERRIES: Omit the thyme and sage. Substitute blue cornmeal for the yellow cornmeal. Fold in $1/2$ cup fresh or frozen (do not thaw) blueberries with the melted butter.

Nutritional Analyses

Herbed Corn Bread Squares (each serving): *About 183 calories (9 percent from protein; 73 percent from carbohydrates; 18 percent from fat), 4 grams protein, 34 grams carbohydrates, 4 grams fat (2 grams saturated fat), 31 milligrams cholesterol, 164 milligrams sodium*

Blue Corn Bread with Blueberries (each serving): *About 188 calories (8 percent from protein; 74 percent from carbohydrates; 18 percent from fat), 4 grams protein, 35 grams carbohydrates, 4 grams fat (2 grams saturated fat), 31 milligrams cholesterol, 164 milligrams sodium*

Old-Fashioned Dried Fruit Loaf

MAKES 12 SERVINGS

· ❋ ·

New Classic Method

Studded with raisins and dates, this moist bread is a variation on my mom's applesauce loaf. Even though its fat has been reduced, it is loaded with old-fashioned flavor.

1 cup unbleached all-purpose flour (*spoon* into measuring cup and level top)
1 cup whole wheat flour (*spoon* into measuring cup and level top)
1 teaspoon baking powder
$\frac{1}{2}$ teaspoon baking soda
$\frac{1}{2}$ teaspoon ground cinnamon
$\frac{1}{8}$ teaspoon salt

$\frac{3}{4}$ cup unsweetened applesauce
$\frac{1}{2}$ cup plus 2 tablespoons packed dark brown sugar
$\frac{1}{4}$ cup 1 percent low-fat milk
1 large egg
2 large egg whites
1 $\frac{1}{2}$ teaspoons canola oil
Grated zest of 1 lemon or $\frac{1}{4}$ teaspoon pure lemon oil

$\frac{1}{4}$ cup raisins
$\frac{1}{4}$ cup chopped pitted dates

1. Position a rack in the center of the oven and preheat to 350° F. Line the bottom of a 9 × 5 × 3-inch nonstick loaf pan with waxed paper, and lightly spray the inside of the pan with oil.

2. In a medium bowl, whisk the flours, baking powder, baking soda, cinnamon, and salt until well combined. Set aside.

3. In another medium bowl, using a handheld electric mixer set at high speed, beat the applesauce, brown sugar, milk, egg, egg whites, oil, and lemon zest until frothy, about 2 minutes. Make a well in the center of the dry ingredients and pour in the applesauce mixture. Using a spoon, stir just until moistened (there should be traces of flour remaining). Add the raisins and dates and stir just until the flour is incorporated. Do not overmix. Using a gentle touch, spread the batter in the prepared pan.

4. Bake until the top of the loaf springs back when pressed gently in the center and the sides are beginning to pull away from the pan, 35 to 40 minutes. Do not overbake. Cool in the pan on a wire cake rack for 10 minutes. Unmold the loaf onto a wire rack and peel off the waxed paper. Turn right side up and cool completely.

Nutritional Analysis

Each serving: *About 158 calories (10 percent calories from protein; 83 percent from carbohydrates; 8 percent from fat), 4 grams protein, 34 grams carbohydrates, 1 gram fat (less than 1 gram saturated fat), 18 milligrams cholesterol, 106 milligrams sodium*

Double Delicious Gingerbread

MAKES 9 SERVINGS

· ❈ ·

New Classic Method

*T*his is the gingerbread to make when you want to serve it warm out of the oven with a cup of hot cider. Crystallized ginger is available in the spice or ethnic food departments at many supermarkets, but the best (yet least expensive) ginger is found in bulk at Asian markets. If you wish, serve the gingerbread with a spoonful of Ginger Custard Sauce (page 141).

Nonstick canola oil spray

1 ½ cups unbleached all-purpose flour (*spoon* into
  measuring cup and level top)
1 cup whole wheat flour (*spoon* into measuring
  cup and level top)
1 tablespoon minced crystallized ginger (optional)
2 teaspoons ground cinnamon
1 ½ teaspoons baking soda
1 teaspoon ground ginger
¼ teaspoon ground cloves
⅛ teaspoon salt

1 cup hot water
1 cup unsulphured molasses
½ cup packed dark brown sugar
½ cup unsweetened applesauce
1 large egg
2 tablespoons canola oil

Confectioners' sugar for sprinkling

1. Position a rack in the center of the oven and preheat to 350° F. Lightly spray an 8-inch square nonstick baking pan with oil.

2. In a medium bowl, whisk the flours, crystallized ginger (if using), cinnamon, baking soda, ground ginger, cloves, and salt until well combined. Set aside.

3. In another medium bowl, using a handheld electric mixer set at high speed, beat the hot water, molasses, brown sugar, applesauce, egg, and oil until frothy, about 2 minutes. Make a well in the center of the dry ingredients, and pour in the liquid. Using a spoon, stir just until combined. Do not overmix. Using a gentle touch, spread the batter evenly in the prepared pan.

4. Bake until the top of the cake springs back when touched gently in the center and the edges are beginning to pull away from the sides of the pan, about 50 minutes. Do not overbake. Cool in the pan on a wire cake rack for 10 minutes. Serve warm, or cool completely in the pan on a wire cake rack. Sift confectioners' sugar over the top.

....

Nutritional Analysis

Each serving: *About 305 calories (6 percent from protein; 82 percent from carbohydrates; 12 percent from fat), 5 grams protein, 64 grams carbohydrates, 4 grams fat (less than 1 gram saturated fat), 24 milligrams cholesterol, 185 milligrams sodium*

Honey Snack Cake

· ✳ ·

New Classic Method

*H*oney is delicious, but sometimes it can overpower a recipe. I find a little ginger tempers its strength. Use a clear, grade A honey for the best flavor. I love the rich, lightly spicy flavor of wildflower honey.

Nonstick canola oil spray

2 cups whole wheat *pastry* flour (*spoon* into
   measuring cup and level top)
1 teaspoon baking soda
$\frac{1}{2}$ teaspoon ground ginger
$\frac{1}{8}$ teaspoon salt

$\frac{3}{4}$ cup honey
$\frac{3}{4}$ cup unsweetened applesauce
$\frac{1}{3}$ cup 1 percent low-fat milk
1 large egg
2 large egg whites
2 tablespoons instant nonfat dry milk powder
   (do not reconstitute)
1 tablespoon canola oil
1 tablespoon vanilla extract

Confectioners' sugar for sprinkling

1. Position a rack in the center of the oven and preheat to 350° F. Lightly spray an 8-inch square nonstick baking pan with oil.

2. In a medium bowl, whisk the flour, baking soda, ginger, and salt until well combined. Set aside.

3. In another medium bowl, using a handheld electric mixer set at

high speed, beat the honey, applesauce, milk, egg, egg whites, instant nonfat dry milk powder, oil, and vanilla until frothy, about 2 minutes. Make a well in the center of the dry ingredients, and pour in the honey mixture. Using a spoon, stir just until combined. Do not overmix. Using a gentle touch, spread the batter evenly in the prepared pan.

4. Bake until the top of the cake springs back when touched gently in the center, about 35 to 40 minutes. Do not overbake. Cool in the pan on a wire cake rack for 10 minutes. Unmold the cake onto the rack, turn right side up, and cool completely. Sift confectioners' sugar over the top.

Nutritional Analysis
Each serving: *About 230 calories (10 percent from protein; 80 percent from carbohydrates; 10 percent from fat), 6 grams protein, 47 grams carbohydrates, 3 grams fat (less than 1 gram saturated fat), 24 milligrams cholesterol, 152 milligrams sodium*

Glazed Lemon Cake

MAKES 9 SERVINGS

· ✳ ·

New Classic Method

$\mathcal{M}$aybe it's the lemon in this recipe, but it always puts me in the mood for a cup of hot tea. If you wish, a small amount of poppy seeds can be added to the dry ingredients. The poppy seeds add a mellow crunch, but they also contain plenty of fat along with their flavor. Store poppy seeds in the freezer, as they go rancid quickly at room temperature.

Nonstick canola oil spray

2 cups unbleached all-purpose flour (*spoon* into
  measuring cup and level top)
2 teaspoons baking powder
$\frac{1}{8}$ teaspoon salt

$\frac{3}{4}$ cup unsweetened applesauce
$\frac{3}{4}$ cup sugar
1 large egg
2 large egg whites
2 tablespoons canola oil
Grated zest of 2 lemons or a generous $\frac{1}{4}$ teaspoon pure
  lemon oil
1 teaspoon vanilla extract

Lemon Glaze (page 140)

1. Position a rack in the center of the oven and preheat to 350° F. Lightly spray an 8-inch square nonstick baking pan with oil.

2. In a medium bowl, whisk the flour, baking powder, and salt until well combined. Set aside.

3. In another medium bowl, using a handheld electric mixer set at high speed, beat the applesauce, sugar, egg, egg whites, oil, lemon zest, and vanilla until frothy, about 2 minutes. Make a well in the center of the dry ingredients and pour in the applesauce mixture. Using a spoon, stir just until combined. Do not overmix. Using a gentle touch, spread the batter into the prepared pan.

4. Bake until the top of the cake springs back when pressed gently in the center and the edges are lightly browned, 30 to 35 minutes. Do not overbake. Cool in the pan on a wire cake rack for 10 minutes. Unmold onto the rack, turn right side up, and cool completely.

5. When cool, glaze the cake with the lemon glaze, letting it drip down the sides. Let stand until the glaze sets.

GLAZED LEMON CAKE WITH POPPY SEEDS: Add 2 tablespoons poppy seeds and whisk with the dry ingredients.

....

Nutritional Analyses
Glazed Lemon Cake (each serving): *About 159 calories (8 percent from protein; 75 percent from carbohydrates; 16 percent from fat), 3 grams protein, 30 grams carbohydrates, 3 grams fat (less than 1 gram saturated fat), 18 milligrams cholesterol, 92 milligrams sodium*
Glazed Lemon Cake with Poppy Seeds (each serving): *About 266 calories (7 percent from protein; 77 percent from carbohydrates; 16 percent from fat), 5 grams protein, 53 grams carbohydrates, 5 grams fat (less than 1 gram saturated fat), 24 milligrams cholesterol, 105 milligrams sodium*

Hot Mocha Pudding Cake

MAKES 9 SERVINGS

· ✳ ·

New Classic Method

Versions of this eggless wonder have been around for ages—the batter separates into a tender chocolate cake with a layer of thick, fudgy mocha sauce underneath. Brown sugar not only enhances the chocolate taste but contributes to the delicious gooeyness. If you have one, bake it in a 9-inch baking pan. But this size pan isn't too common, so I make mine in an 8-inch pan set on a baking sheet to catch any drips. Serve it hot, warm, or even cold, either plain or with a big scoop of vanilla frozen yogurt.

CAKE

    1 cup unbleached all-purpose flour (*spoon* into measuring cup and level top)

    2 teaspoons baking powder

    $\frac{1}{8}$ teaspoon salt

    $\frac{3}{4}$ cup granulated sugar

    $\frac{1}{2}$ cup 1 percent low-fat milk

    3 tablespoons Dutch-process cocoa powder

    2 tablespoons canola oil

    1 $\frac{1}{2}$ teaspoons espresso powder

TOPPING

    $\frac{3}{4}$ cup packed dark brown sugar

    3 tablespoons Dutch-process cocoa powder

    1 $\frac{3}{4}$ cups boiling water

1. Position a rack in the center of the oven and preheat to 350° F.

2. In a medium bowl, whisk the flour, baking powder, and salt until well combined. Set aside.

3. In another medium bowl, using a handheld electric mixer set at high speed, beat the sugar, milk, cocoa, oil, and espresso powder until the mixture is frothy, about 2 minutes. Make a well in the center of the dry ingredients, and pour in the milk mixture. Stir with a spoon just until combined. Spread into an ungreased 8-inch square nonstick baking pan.

4. To make the topping, combine the brown sugar and cocoa powder in a small bowl. Sprinkle evenly over the top of the batter, then pour the boiling water over all. Place the pan on an aluminum foil–lined baking sheet, just in case the mixture boils over in the oven.

5. Bake until a cake layer forms in the pan, and the top springs back when touched lightly in the center, about 40 minutes. Serve hot or warm, spooned into bowls.

Nutritional Analysis

Each serving: *About 212 calories (5 percent from protein; 81 percent from carbohydrates; 15 percent from fat), 3 grams protein, 46 grams carbohydrates, 4 grams fat (less than 1 gram saturated fat), less than 1 gram cholesterol, 114 milligrams sodium*

Fresh Papaya Loaf

MAKES 12 SERVINGS

· ✻ ·

New Classic Method

This golden loaf has the tropical taste of the islands. A ripe papaya will "give" when squeezed gently, and have a rich, fruity aroma. To prepare the papaya, peel with a vegetable peeler or a small sharp knife. Cut it in half and discard the small black seeds.

Nonstick canola oil spray

1 cup unbleached all-purpose flour (*spoon* into measuring cup and level top)

1 cup whole wheat flour (*spoon* into measuring cup and level top)

1 teaspoon baking soda

$\frac{1}{8}$ teaspoon salt

1 cup sugar

$\frac{3}{4}$ cup unsweetened applesauce

$\frac{1}{2}$ cup low-fat buttermilk

1 large egg

2 large egg whites

1 tablespoon canola oil

Grated zest of 1 lemon or $\frac{1}{4}$ teaspoon pure lemon oil

1 cup ($\frac{3}{4}$-inch dice) ripe papaya chunks (about 1 medium papaya)

1. Position a rack in the center of the oven and preheat to 350° F. Line the bottom of a 9 × 5 × 3-inch nonstick loaf pan with waxed paper and lightly spray the inside of the pan with oil.

2. In a medium bowl, whisk the flours, baking soda, and salt until well combined. Set aside.

3. In another medium bowl, using a handheld electric mixer set at high speed, beat the sugar, applesauce, buttermilk, egg, egg whites, oil, and lemon zest until frothy, about 2 minutes. Make a well in the center of the dry ingredients and pour in the applesauce mixture. Using a spoon, stir just until moistened (there should be traces of flour remaining). Add the papaya chunks and stir just until the flour is incorporated. Do not overmix. Using a gentle touch, spread the batter in the prepared pan.

4. Bake until the top of the loaf springs back when pressed gently in the center and the sides are beginning to pull away from the pan, 55 to 60 minutes. Do not overbake. Cool in the pan on a wire cake rack for 10 minutes. Unmold onto a wire cake rack. Peel off the waxed paper. Turn right side up and cool completely.

Nutritional Analysis
Each serving: *About 166 calories (9 percent from protein; 81 percent from carbohydrates; 10 percent from fat), 4 grams protein, 35 grams carbohydrates, 2 grams fat (less than 1 gram saturated fat), 18 milligrams cholesterol, 117 milligrams sodium*

Peach Upside-Down Cake

MAKES 9 SERVINGS

· ✳ ·

New Classic Method

Like many busy moms, I always seem to have some kind of canned fruit in the house to turn into a quick lunch with some yogurt or cottage cheese. I use canned fruit for impromptu baking too, when I can't get to the store to buy fresh fruit. Peach halves are a snap to turn into a great upside-down cake with ingredients I always have in my pantry. (I hate to say it, but sometimes canned peaches are more reliable than fresh. Don't get me wrong—nothing beats summery peaches from a local farm, but winter's tasteless imported peaches will do nothing for your baked goods.)

Nonstick canola oil spray

PEACH LAYER
6 canned peach halves in water, drained
$^1/_4$ cup packed dark brown sugar
2 tablespoons applesauce
1 tablespoon unsalted butter, melted
$^1/_2$ teaspoon ground cinnamon

CAKE LAYER
1 $^1/_2$ cups whole wheat *pastry* flour (*spoon* into measuring cup and level top)
1 teaspoon ground cinnamon
$^3/_4$ teaspoon baking soda
$^1/_8$ teaspoon salt

1 $^1/_2$ cups low-fat buttermilk
$^1/_2$ cup packed dark brown sugar
1 large egg
2 teaspoons canola oil
1 teaspoon vanilla extract

1. Position a rack in the center of the oven and preheat to 350° F. Lightly spray an 8-inch square nonstick baking pan with oil.

2. To prepare the peach layer, drain the peach halves well on paper towels. Place, cut side down, in the prepared pan. In a small bowl, combine the brown sugar, applesauce, melted butter, and cinnamon. Sprinkle over the peaches. Set the pan aside.

3. In a medium bowl, whisk the flour, cinnamon, baking soda, and salt until well combined. Set aside.

4. In another medium bowl, using a handheld electric mixer set at high speed, beat the buttermilk, brown sugar, egg, oil, and vanilla until frothy, about 2 minutes. Make a well in the center of the dry ingredients and pour in the buttermilk mixture. Using a spoon, stir just until combined. Do not overmix. Using a gentle touch, spread the batter over the peach layer.

5. Bake until the top of the cake springs back when pressed gently in the center and the sides are beginning to pull away from the pan, 45 to 50 minutes. Cool in the pan on a wire cake rack for 5 minutes only. Run a knife around the inside of the pan. Using a kitchen towel to protect your hands, carefully unmold the cake onto a rimmed serving plate so the fruit is on top. (There will be a lot of hot juices, so be careful.) If any of the fruit remains in the pan, transfer it to the top of the cake. Serve warm.

....

Nutritional Analysis
Each serving: *About 195 calories (10 percent from protein; 74 percent from carbohydrates; 16 percent from fat), 5 grams protein, 37 grams carbohydrates, 4 grams fat (less than 1 gram saturated fat), 29 milligrams cholesterol, 155 milligrams sodium*

Persimmon Yogurt Loaf

MAKES 12 SERVINGS

· ❋ ·

New Classic Method

Growing up in California, we had a Hachiya persimmon tree. This persimmon has bright orange, heart-shaped fruit, and must be thoroughly ripened until very soft, or it will be inedibly tannic. Don't confuse Hachiyas with Fuyu persimmons, a squat variety that can be eaten when still firm. The persimmon puree makes a delicious loaf with pumpkin-like flavor, and is especially delicious with a scoop of frozen vanilla yogurt. If desired, give the baked loaf a finishing touch with a drizzle of Lemon Glaze (page 140).

Nonstick canola oil spray

1 cup unbleached all-purpose flour (*spoon* into
    measuring cup and level top)
1 cup whole wheat flour (*spoon* into measuring
    cup and level top)
1 ¹/₂ teaspoons baking soda
1 ¹/₂ teaspoons ground cinnamon
¹/₂ teaspoon freshly grated nutmeg
¹/₈ teaspoon salt

³/₄ cup persimmon puree (1 large, soft-ripe
    Hachiya persimmon)
¹/₄ cup unsweetened applesauce, as needed
1 cup sugar
¹/₂ cup plain nonfat yogurt
1 large egg
1 tablespoon canola oil
Grated zest of 1 lemon or ¹/₄ teaspoon pure lemon oil
2 tablespoons fresh lemon juice

1. Position a rack in the center of the oven and preheat to 350° F. Line the bottom of a 9 × 5 × 3-inch loaf pan with waxed paper and lightly spray the inside of the pan with oil.

2. In a medium bowl, whisk the flours, baking soda, cinnamon, nutmeg, and salt until well combined. Set aside.

3. Wash and then coarsely chop the persimmon (no need to peel), removing the stem. In a food processor fitted with the metal blade or in a blender, puree the persimmon. You should have about ¾ cup puree. Add ¼ cup applesauce as needed to make 1 cup of the persimmon/applesauce mixture.

4. In another medium bowl, using a handheld electric mixer set at high speed, beat the 1 cup persimmon/applesauce mixture, sugar, yogurt, egg, oil, lemon zest, and lemon juice until frothy, about 2 minutes. Make a well in the center of the dry ingredients and pour in the persimmon mixture. Using a spoon, stir just until smooth. Do not overmix. Using a gentle touch, spread the batter in the prepared pan.

5. Bake until the top of the loaf springs back when pressed gently in the center, and the sides are beginning to pull away from the pan, 45 to 50 minutes. Do not overbake. Cool in the pan on a wire cake rack for 10 minutes. Unmold the loaf onto the wire cake rack and peel off the waxed paper. Turn right side up and cool completely.

Nutritional Analysis

Each serving: *About 165 calories (8 percent from protein; 82 percent from carbohydrates; 10 percent from fat), 4 grams protein, 35 grams carbohydrates, 2 grams fat (less than 1 gram saturated fat), 18 milligrams cholesterol, 139 milligrams sodium*

Grandma's Pineapple Upside-Down Skillet Cake

MAKES 10 SERVINGS

· ❈ ·

New Classic Method

*T*he mark of a successful reduced-fat cake is when your family says they can't tell the difference from Grandma's old recipe. That's what happened when I served my take on my husband's great-grandma Brugge's heirloom upside-down cake.

PINEAPPLE LAYER
One 20-ounce can pineapple rings in juice, drained, juice reserved
2 tablespoons unsalted butter
1/2 cup packed dark brown sugar

CAKE LAYER
1 cup unbleached all-purpose flour (*spoon* into measuring cup and level top)
1 teaspoon baking powder
1/8 teaspoon salt

1/2 cup packed dark brown sugar
1/3 cup plus 1 tablespoon reserved pineapple juice (and/or water)
1 large egg
4 large egg whites

1. Position a rack in the center of the oven and preheat to 350° F. Wrap the handle of a 10-inch nonstick skillet with aluminum foil, or use an ovenproof skillet. (Measure the skillet across the top.)

2. To prepare the pineapple layer, dry the drained pineapple rings well on paper towels. In the skillet over medium heat, melt the butter. Add the brown sugar and stir until completely melted. Cook, stirring often, until thick and syrupy, about 1 minute. Remove from the heat. Arrange the pineapple rings in the syrup.

3. To make the cake, in a medium bowl, whisk the flour, baking powder, and salt until well combined. Set aside.

4. In another medium bowl, using a handheld electric mixer set at high speed, beat the brown sugar, pineapple juice, egg, and egg whites until frothy, about 2 minutes. Make a well in the center of the dry ingredients and pour in the pineapple juice mixture. Using a spoon, stir just until combined. Do not overmix. Using a gentle touch, spread the batter over the pineapple layer.

5. Bake until the top of the cake is lightly browned and springs back when pressed gently in the center, about 20 minutes. Do not overbake. Cool in the pan on a wire cake rack for 5 minutes. Run a knife around the inside of the skillet. Using a kitchen towel to protect your hands, carefully unmold the cake onto a rimmed serving plate so the fruit is on top (there will be some hot juices in the skillet, so be careful). If any of the fruit remains in the skillet, transfer it to the top of the cake. Serve warm.

Nutritional Analysis

Each serving: *About 190 calories (7 percent from protein; 78 percent from carbohydrates; 14 percent from fat), 4 grams protein, 38 grams carbohydrates, 3 grams fat (2 grams saturated fat), 28 milligrams cholesterol, 96 milligrams sodium*

Pumpkin-Chocolate Chip Ring

MAKES 10 SERVINGS

· ※ ·

New Classic Method

Here I've combined three of my favorite flavors—pumpkin, orange, and chocolate chips. They create a flavorful cake that cuts into firm slices and is perfect for entertaining.

Nonstick canola oil spray

1 ¼ cups whole wheat *pastry* flour (*spoon* into
   measuring cup and level top)
½ teaspoon baking soda
½ teaspoon ground cinnamon
Pinch of freshly grated nutmeg
Pinch of salt

⅓ cup plus 1 tablespoon canned pumpkin
¼ cup unsweetened applesauce
Grated zest of 1 orange or ¼ teaspoon pure orange oil
¼ cup fresh orange juice or water
3 tablespoons packed dark brown sugar
1 large egg
1 ½ teaspoons canola oil
1 teaspoon vanilla extract

⅓ cup mini-chocolate chips

1 tablespoon confectioners' sugar

1. Position a rack in the center of the oven and preheat to 350° F. Generously spray a 6-cup nonstick fluted tube cake pan with oil.

2. In a medium bowl, whisk the flour, baking soda, cinnamon, nutmeg, and salt until well combined. Set aside.

3. In another medium bowl, using a handheld electric mixer set at high speed, beat the pumpkin, applesauce, orange zest, orange juice, brown sugar, egg, oil, and vanilla until light and frothy, about 2 minutes. Make a well in the center of the dry ingredients and pour in the pumpkin mixture. Using a spoon, stir just until moistened (there should be wisps of flour remaining). Add the chocolate chips and stir just until smooth. Do not overmix. Using a gentle touch, spread the batter in the prepared pan.

4. Bake until the top of the cake springs back when pressed gently in the center and the sides are beginning to pull away from the pan, about 30 minutes. Do not overbake. Cool in the pan on a wire cake rack for 10 minutes. Unmold the cake onto the wire cake rack and cool completely. Sprinkle the confectioners' sugar over the cooled cake.

Nutritional Analysis

Each serving: *About 124 calories (9 percent from protein; 69 percent from carbohydrates; 21 percent from fat), 3 grams protein, 23 grams carbohydrates, 3 grams fat (less than 1 gram saturated fat), 21 milligrams cholesterol, 71 milligrams sodium*

Pumpkin-Orange Corn Bread

MAKES 12 SERVINGS

· ✺ ·

New Classic Method

I first came to appreciate Native American culture as a teenager, and spent a summer as an apprentice to the well-known silversmith Lawrence Saufkie and his family in Second Mesa, Arizona. In addition to polishing my silversmithing skills, I also learned how to grind maize and make all kinds of cornmeal dishes. I still love anything with cornmeal, and I consider this hearty pumpkin corn bread my signature dish. It always graces my Thanksgiving dessert table. If you wish, fold ½ cup coarsely chopped roasted pumpkin seeds and ½ cup chopped pitted dates into the batter.

Nonstick canola oil spray

1 cup unbleached all-purpose flour (*spoon* into
   measuring cup and level top)
1 cup yellow cornmeal, preferably stone-ground
1 teaspoon baking soda
1 teaspoon ground cinnamon
1 teaspoon freshly grated nutmeg
½ teaspoon ground ginger
¼ teaspoon ground cloves
⅛ teaspoon salt

1 cup canned pumpkin
1 cup packed dark brown sugar
1 cup low-fat buttermilk
1 large egg
Grated zest of 1 orange or ¼ teaspoon pure orange oil
1 tablespoon canola oil

1. Position a rack in the center of the oven and preheat to 350° F. Line the bottom of a 9 × 5 × 3-inch nonstick loaf pan with waxed paper and lightly spray the inside of the pan with oil.

2. In a medium bowl, whisk the flour, cornmeal, baking soda, cinnamon, nutmeg, ginger, cloves, and salt until well combined. Set aside.

3. In another medium bowl, using a handheld electric mixer set at high speed, beat the pumpkin, brown sugar, buttermilk, egg, orange zest, and oil until lightened and frothy, about 2 minutes. Make a well in the center of the dry ingredients and pour in the pumpkin mixture. Using a spoon, stir just until combined. Do not overmix. Using a gentle touch, spread the batter in the prepared pan.

4. Bake until the top of the corn bread springs back when pressed gently in the center and the sides are beginning to pull away from the pan, 55 to 60 minutes. Do not overbake. Cool in the pan on a wire cake rack for 10 minutes. Unmold the cake onto a wire cake rack and peel off the waxed paper. Turn right side up and cool completely.

. . . .

Nutritional Analysis

Each serving: *About 182 calories (8 percent from protein; 82 percent from carbohydrates; 11 percent from fat), 4 grams protein, 38 grams carbohydrates, 2 grams fat (less than 1 gram saturated fat), 19 milligrams cholesterol, 125 milligrams sodium*

Raisin Bran Loaf

MAKES 12 SERVINGS

· ✻ ·

New Classic Method

The wholesome goodness of this loaf is evident in every bite. A bit of orange zest adds another layer of flavor that I love. Raisins are full of fiber and iron.

Nonstick canola oil spray

2 cups whole wheat flour (*spoon* into measuring
    cup and level top)
1/2 cup unprocessed (miller's) wheat bran
1 teaspoon baking soda
1 teaspoon ground cinnamon
1/2 teaspoon salt

3/4 cup unsweetened applesauce
3/4 cup low-fat buttermilk
1/2 cup packed dark brown sugar
1 large egg
1 teaspoon vanilla extract
Grated zest of 1 orange or 1/4 teaspoon pure orange oil

1/2 cup raisins

1. Position a rack in the center of the oven and preheat to 350° F. Line the bottom of a 9 × 5 × 3-inch nonstick loaf pan with waxed paper and lightly spray the inside of the pan with oil.

2. In a medium bowl, whisk the flour, bran, baking soda, cinnamon, and salt until well combined. Set aside.

3. In another medium bowl, using a handheld electric mixer set at high speed, beat the applesauce, buttermilk, brown sugar, egg, vanilla, and orange zest until frothy, about 2 minutes. Make a well in the center of the dry ingredients and pour in the applesauce mixture. Using a spoon, stir just until moistened (there should be wisps of flour remaining). Add the raisins and stir just until smooth. Do not overmix. Using a gentle touch, spread the batter in the prepared pan.

4. Bake until the top of the loaf springs back when pressed gently in the center and the sides are beginning to pull away from the pan, 35 to 40 minutes. Cool in the pan on a wire cake rack for 10 minutes. Unmold the loaf onto a wire rack and peel off the waxed paper. Turn right side up and cool completely.

Nutritional Analysis

Each serving: *About 146 calories (11 percent from protein; 83 percent from carbohydrates; 6 percent from fat), 4 grams protein, 33 grams carbohydrates, 1 gram fat (less than 1 gram saturated fat), 18 milligrams cholesterol, 117 milligrams sodium*

Spicy Salsa Scones

MAKES 8 SCONES

· ❋ ·

*M*ost scone recipes have a stick of butter in them—way too much for my taste. These have half the amount of typical recipes, and a very untypical kick from salsa. Use your favorite thick and chunky brand salsa from a jar (it just doesn't work as well with homemade or refrigerated fresh salsa). I've used everything from standard-issue red tomato and chile, to green tomatillo, to black bean and corn. The dough should resemble soft, moist biscuit dough. If it seems too sticky (caused by excess liquid in the salsa), work in a little more flour, but be careful not to overhandle the dough.

Nonstick canola oil spray

1 ½ cups unbleached all-purpose flour (*spoon* into
    measuring cup and level top)
½ cup whole wheat flour (*spoon* into measuring cup
    and level top)
1 teaspoon baking soda
⅛ teaspoon salt
⅛ teaspoon cayenne pepper (optional)
4 tablespoons (½ stick) unsalted butter, chilled, cut
    into ½-inch pieces

½ cup medium-hot, thick and chunky salsa *from a jar*
1 large egg (do not use 2 egg whites)
3 tablespoons instant nonfat dry milk powder (do not
    reconstitute)

1. Position a rack in the center of the oven and preheat to 350° F. Lightly spray an 8-inch round nonstick cake pan with oil.

2. In a medium bowl, whisk the flour, baking soda, salt, and cayenne, if using it, until well combined. Using a pastry blender, cut in the butter until the mixture resembles coarse crumbs.

3. In a small bowl, whisk the salsa, egg, and milk powder to combine. Make a well in the center of the dry ingredients and pour in the salsa mixture. Using a spoon, stir just until combined. Knead briefly in the bowl until the dough comes together. Transfer to the prepared pan and evenly pat out. Using a large knife, score the dough into 8 wedges.

4. Bake until the center feels firm when pressed gently and the edges are golden brown, about 25 minutes. Do not overbake. Cool in the pan on a wire cake rack for 10 minutes. Serve warm, or cool completely in the pan on a wire cake rack.

Nutritional Analysis
Each scone: *About 189 calories (10 percent from protein; 58 percent from carbohydrates; 32 percent from fat), 5 grams protein, 27 grams carbohydrates, 7 grams fat (4 grams saturated fat), 42 milligrams cholesterol, 308 milligrams sodium*

Whole Wheat Date Cake

MAKES 9 SERVINGS

· ❋ ·

New Classic Method

*D*ates add a luscious sweetness to baked goods and also add potassium, iron, and fiber. Precut dates are fine, but they can be a bit dry. It's better to cut up pitted dates with a large, sharp knife that has been sprayed with nonstick canola oil spray. They can also be pulsed in a food processor until chopped. Whole wheat flours adds fiber, too.

Nonstick canola oil spray

1 ½ cups unbleached all-purpose flour (*spoon* into
   measuring cup and level top)
1 cup whole wheat flour (*spoon* into measuring
   cup and level top)
2 teaspoons baking powder
1 teaspoon baking soda
1 teaspoon ground cinnamon
⅛ teaspoon salt

1 cup packed dark brown sugar
¾ cup unsweetened applesauce
1 large egg
2 large egg whites
1 tablespoon canola oil
2 teaspoons vanilla extract

Grated zest of 1 orange or ¼ teaspoon pure orange oil
½ cup chopped pitted dates

1. Position a rack in the center of the oven and preheat to 350° F. Lightly spray an 8-inch square nonstick baking pan with oil.

2. In a medium bowl, whisk the flours, baking powder, baking soda, cinnamon, and salt until well combined. Set aside.

3. In another medium bowl, using a handheld electric mixer set at high speed, beat the brown sugar, applesauce, egg, egg whites, oil, vanilla, and orange zest until frothy, about 2 minutes. Make a well in the center of the dry ingredients and pour in the applesauce mixture. Using a spoon, stir just until moistened (there should be few wisps of flour remaining). Add the dates and stir just until the batter is smooth. Do not overmix. Using a gentle touch, spread the batter evenly in the prepared pan.

4. Bake until the top of the cake springs back when touched gently in the center and the sides are beginning to pull away from the pan, 35 to 40 minutes. Do not overbake. Cool in the pan on a wire cake rack for 10 minutes. Unmold onto the rack, turn right side up, and cool completely.

Nutritional Analysis

Each serving: *About 280 calories (8 percent from protein; 84 percent from carbohydrates; 8 percent from fat), 6 grams protein, 60 grams carbohydrates, 3 grams fat (less than 1 gram saturated fat), 24 milligrams cholesterol, 222 milligrams sodium*

Zucchini Tea Loaf

· ❋ ·

New Classic Method

*E*very baker needs a good zucchini bread recipe. Not only do I bake this for snacking and lunch boxes but also for holiday gift-giving.

Nonstick canola oil spray

1 cup unbleached all-purpose flour (*spoon* into
     measuring cup and level top)
1 cup whole wheat flour (*spoon* into measuring
     cup and level top)
1 teaspoon baking soda
$\frac{1}{8}$ teaspoon salt

1 cup packed dark brown sugar
$\frac{3}{4}$ cup unsweetened applesauce
$\frac{1}{2}$ cup low-fat buttermilk
1 large egg
2 large egg whites
1 tablespoon canola oil
1 teaspoon vanilla extract
Grated zest of 1 lemon or $\frac{1}{4}$ teaspoon pure lemon oil

1 cup shredded zucchini

1. Position a rack in the center of the oven and preheat to 350° F. Line the bottom of a 9 × 5 × 3-inch nonstick loaf pan with waxed paper and lightly spray the inside of the pan with oil.

2. In a medium bowl, whisk the flours, baking soda, and salt until well combined. Set aside.

3. In another medium bowl, using a handheld electric mixer set at high speed, beat the brown sugar, applesauce, buttermilk, egg, egg whites, oil, vanilla, and lemon zest until frothy, about 2 minutes. Make a well in the center of the dry ingredients and pour in the applesauce mixture. Using a spoon, stir just until moistened. The batter will be thick, and there should be wisps of flour remaining. Add the zucchini and stir just until the flour is incorporated. Do not overmix. Using a gentle touch, spread the batter in the prepared pan.

4. Bake until the top of the loaf springs back when pressed gently in the center and the sides are beginning to pull away from the pan, 55 to 60 minutes. Do not overbake. Cool in the pan on a wire cake rack in the pan for 10 minutes. Unmold the loaf onto a wire rack and peel off the waxed paper. Turn right side up and cool completely.

Nutritional Analysis
Each serving: *About 173 calories (9 percent from protein; 81 percent from carbohydrates; 10 percent from fat), 4 grams protein, 36 grams carbohydrates, 2 grams fat (less than 1 gram saturated fat), 18 milligrams cholesterol, 123 milligrams sodium*

New Cake Classics:
Layer Cakes and
Cheesecakes for
Special Occasions with
Frostings, Glazes,
and Sauces

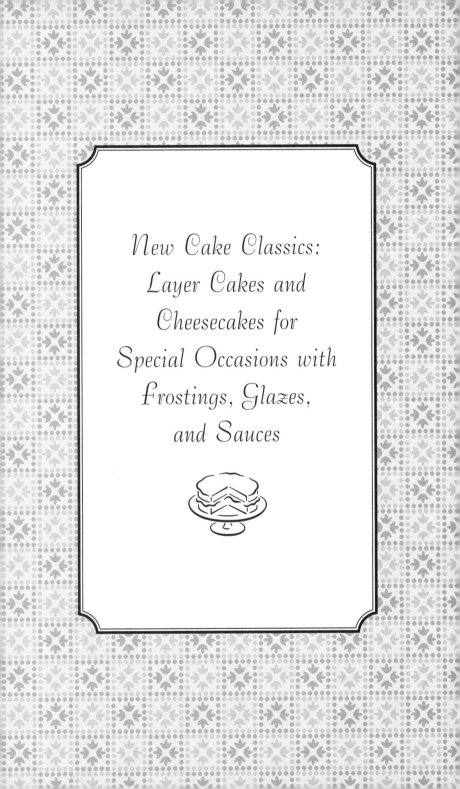

Orange Angel Food Cake

MAKES 16 SERVINGS

· 🎇 ·

One of America's favorite cakes has always been nonfat. Angel food cake drizzled with Orange Glaze (page 140) and topped with fresh mandarin orange or grapefruit sections has become a New Year's tradition at our house. Here are a few tips for a perfect angel food cake. First, if you have a heavy-duty electric mixer, it makes short work of beating the egg whites, but a hand mixer works well, too. Be sure that the egg whites are completely free of any trace of egg yolk. Sift the cake flour over the beaten egg white so it incorporates more easily. Don't grease the pan—the batter needs to "climb" up a tactile surface. And never try to make angel food cake (or any meringue-based dessert) on a humid day.

> 12 large egg whites, at room temperature (see page 253)
> $1/8$ teaspoon salt
> 1 $1/4$ cups sugar
> Grated zest of 1 orange or $1/4$ teaspoon pure orange oil
> 1 tablespoon fresh orange juice
> 1 cup cake flour, not self-rising (*spoon* into measuring
>   cup and level top)

1. Position a rack in the center of the oven and preheat to 325°F.

2. In a large bowl, using a handheld mixer set at medium speed, beat the egg whites until foamy. Add the salt and increase the speed to high. Beat until the egg whites form very soft peaks. Gradually beat in the sugar, beating until the whites are stiff and glossy. Do not overbeat. Beat in the orange zest and juice.

3. Sift flour over the meringue. Using a large rubber spatula, fold the flour and meringue together. Do not overmix. Using a gentle touch, transfer the batter to an ungreased 10-inch tube pan (preferably *not* nonstick).

4. Bake until the top of the cake is golden brown and springs back when pressed gently in the center, 40 to 50 minutes. Invert the cake pan (if the cake pan doesn't have feet to keep the cake from touching the surface, invert the cake in pan on a standing bottle or funnel) and let stand until the cake is completely cooled.

5. Using a metal icing spatula or a long serrated knife, carefully loosen the cake from the sides of the pan and place it on a serving platter. To serve, slice with a serrated knife.

N o t e : Rather than crack open a dozen eggs, I prefer to use dried egg whites (page 254) to make an angel food cake. Carefully follow the reconstituting instructions on the package.

VANILLA ANGEL FOOD CAKE: Substitute 1 $\frac{1}{2}$ teaspoons vanilla extract and $\frac{1}{2}$ teaspoon almond extract for the orange zest and juice.

COCOA-ORANGE ANGEL FOOD CAKE: Substitute $\frac{3}{4}$ cup cake flour and $\frac{1}{4}$ cup Dutch-process cocoa powder for the 1 cup cake flour. Sift the flour and cocoa together. Add 1 teaspoon vanilla extract with the orange juice.

SPICED ANGEL FOOD CAKE: Sift 1 teaspoon ground cinnamon, $\frac{1}{2}$ teaspoon freshly grated nutmeg, and $\frac{1}{4}$ teaspoon ground cloves with the cake flour. Substitute 1 teaspoon vanilla extract for the orange juice and zest.

....

Nutritional Analyses

Orange Angel Food Cake (each serving): *About 95 calories (13 percent from protein; 87 percent from carbohydrates; 0 percent from fat), 3 grams protein, 21 grams carbohydrates, 0 grams fat (0 grams saturated fat), 0 milligrams cholesterol, 58 milligrams sodium*
Vanilla Angel Food Cake (each serving): *About 96 calories (13 percent from protein; 87 percent from carbohydrates; 0 percent from fat), 3 grams protein, 21 grams carbohydrates, 0 grams fat (0 grams saturated fat), 0 milligrams cholesterol, 58 milligrams sodium*
Cocoa Angel Food Cake (each serving): *About 91 calories (14 percent from protein; 85 percent from carbohydrates; 1 percent from fat), 3 grams protein, 21 grams carbohydrates, 0 grams fat (0 grams saturated fat), 0 milligrams cholesterol, 59 milligrams sodium*
Spiced Angel Food Cake (each serving): *About 96 calories (13 percent from protein; 87 percent from carbohydrates; 0 percent from fat), 3 grams protein, 22 grams carbohydrates, 0 grams fat (0 grams saturated fat), 0 milligrams cholesterol, 58 milligrams sodium*

Applesauce Layer Cake

MAKES 12 SERVINGS

· ❈ ·

New Classic Method

*H*ere's another old family recipe that I lightened to reflect today's preference for healthy baking. It's wonderful plain, but if you like, stir in ¼ cup chopped walnuts or ½ cup dried currants (being careful not to overmix the batter).

Nonstick canola oil spray

2 ½ cups whole wheat *pastry* flour (*spoon* into
    measuring cup and level top)
1 ½ teaspoons baking soda
1 teaspoon ground cinnamon
½ teaspoon freshly grated nutmeg
⅛ teaspoon salt

1 cup packed dark brown sugar
¾ cup low-fat buttermilk
¾ cup unsweetened applesauce
1 large egg
2 large egg whites
1 tablespoon canola oil
2 teaspoons vanilla extract

Apple Buttercream Frosting (page 137)

1. Position a rack in the center of the oven and preheat to 350° F. Lightly spray two 8-inch round nonstick cake pans with oil.

2. In a medium bowl, whisk the flour, baking soda, cinnamon, nutmeg, and salt until well combined. Set aside.

3. In another medium bowl, using a handheld electric mixer set at

high speed, beat the brown sugar, buttermilk, applesauce, egg, egg whites, oil, and vanilla until lightened and frothy, about 2 minutes. Make a well in the center of the dry ingredients, and pour in the buttermilk mixture. Using a spoon, stir just until combined. Do not overmix. Divide the batter equally between the prepared pans. Using a gentle touch, smooth the tops.

4. Bake until the top of the cakes springs back when pressed gently in the center and the sides are pulling away from the pans, 25 to 30 minutes. Do not overbake. Cool in the pans on wire cake racks for 10 minutes. Unmold onto the racks, turn right side up, and cool completely.

5. Place one cake, flat side up, on a serving platter. Spread with about ½ cup frosting. Place the other layer, round side up, on the bottom layer. Frost the top of the cake with the remaining icing and serve.

APPLESAUCE SHEET CAKE: Position a rack in the center of the oven and preheat to 350° F. Lightly spray a 9 × 13-inch baking pan with oil. Make the batter according to the recipe instructions. Turn the batter into the prepared pan and gently smooth the top. Bake until the top of the cake springs back when lightly pressed in the center and the edges are beginning to pull away from the sides of the pan, about 25 minutes. Cool completely in the pan on a wire cake rack. If desired, sift 1 tablespoon confectioners' sugar over the top before serving. Makes 15 servings.

Nutritional Analyses

Applesauce Layer Cake (with frosting, each serving): *About 325 calories (8 percent from protein; 83 percent from carbohydrates; 10 percent from fat), 6 grams protein, 69 grams carbohydrates, 4 grams fat (1 gram saturated fat), 22 milligrams cholesterol, 164 milligrams sodium*
Applesauce Sheet Cake (unfrosted, each serving): *About 156 calories (10 percent from protein; 80 percent from carbohydrates; 10 percent from fat), 4 grams protein, 32 grams carbohydrates, 2 grams fat (less than 1 gram saturated fat), 15 milligrams cholesterol, 129 milligrams sodium*

Banana-Raisin Layer Cake

· 🌟 ·

New Classic Method

*M*ost banana cakes are baked in a loaf pan, but this is such a favorite at my house that it often makes an appearance at family celebrations dressed up as a layer cake. If you have the time, the cake tastes even better if the layers are wrapped and refrigerated overnight so the flavors get a chance to mix and mellow.

Nonstick canola oil spray

2 $\frac{1}{2}$ cups whole wheat *pastry* flour (*spoon* into
    measuring cup and level top)
1 $\frac{1}{2}$ teaspoons baking soda
1 teaspoon ground cinnamon
$\frac{1}{2}$ teaspoon freshly grated nutmeg
$\frac{1}{8}$ teaspoon salt

1 cup mashed ripe bananas (about 2 large bananas)
1 cup packed dark brown sugar
$\frac{3}{4}$ cup low-fat buttermilk
$\frac{1}{4}$ cup unsweetened applesauce
1 large egg
2 large egg whites
2 tablespoons canola oil
2 teaspoons vanilla extract

$\frac{1}{2}$ cup golden raisins

Mocha Buttercream Frosting (page 137)

1. Position a rack in the center of the oven and preheat to 350° F. Lightly spray two 8-inch round nonstick cake pans with oil.

2. In a medium bowl, whisk the flour, baking soda, cinnamon, nutmeg, and salt until well combined. Set aside.

3. In another medium bowl, using a handheld electric mixer set at high speed, beat the bananas, brown sugar, buttermilk, applesauce, egg, egg whites, oil, and vanilla until lightened and frothy, about 2 minutes. Make a well in the center of the dry ingredients and pour in the buttermilk mixture. Using a spoon, stir just until moistened (there should be a few traces of flour remaining). Add the raisins and fold in just until the flour is incorporated. Do not overmix. Divide the batter equally between the prepared pans. Using a gentle touch, smooth the tops.

4. Bake until the cakes springs back when pressed gently in the center and the sides are pulling away from the pans, 25 to 30 minutes. Do not overbake. Cool in the pans on wire cake racks for 10 minutes. Unmold onto the racks, turn right side up, and cool completely. If time permits, wrap each layer in plastic wrap and refrigerate overnight.

5. Place one cake, flat side up, on a serving platter. Spread with about ¹/₂ cup frosting. Place the other layer, round side up, on the bottom layer. Frost the top of the cake with the remaining icing and serve.

BANANA-RAISIN SHEET CAKE: Position a rack in the center of the oven and preheat to 350° F. Lightly spray a 9 × 13-inch baking pan with oil. Make the batter according to the recipe instructions. Turn the batter into the prepared pan and gently smooth the top. Bake until the top of the cake springs back when lightly pressed in the center and the edges are beginning to pull away from the sides of the pan, about 25 minutes. Cool completely in the pan on a wire cake rack. If desired, sift 1 tablespoon confectioners' sugar over the top before serving. Makes 15 servings.

Nutritional Analyses

Banana-Raisin Layer Cake (with frosting, each serving): *About 363 calories (7 percent from protein; 81 percent from carbohydrates; 12 percent from fat), 7 grams protein, 76 grams carbohydrates, 5 grams fat (1 gram saturated fat), 22 milligrams cholesterol, 165 milligrams sodium*
Banana-Raisin Sheet Cake (unfrosted, each serving): *About 191 calories (9 percent from protein; 79 percent from carbohydrates; 12 percent from fat), 4 grams protein, 39 grams carbohydrates, 3 grams fat (less than 1 gram saturated fat), 15 milligrams cholesterol, 130 milligrams sodium*

Carrot-Pineapple Layer Cake

MAKES 12 SERVINGS

· ✳ ·

New Class Method

Carrot cake has been a family favorite for years. We used to make Mom's recipe (with a cup of vegetable oil, which contains 218 grams of fat), but this lighter version is our first choice now.

Nonstick canola oil spray

2 $\frac{1}{2}$ cups whole wheat *pastry* flour (*spoon* into
    measuring cup and level top)
1 $\frac{1}{2}$ teaspoons baking soda
1 teaspoon ground cinnamon
$\frac{1}{8}$ teaspoon salt

$\frac{1}{2}$ cup drained, crushed pineapple (from one
    8-ounce can), juice reserved for the frosting
1 cup packed dark brown sugar
$\frac{3}{4}$ cup low-fat buttermilk
$\frac{3}{4}$ cup unsweetened applesauce
1 large egg
2 large egg whites
1 tablespoon canola oil
Grated zest of 1 orange or $\frac{1}{4}$ teaspoon pure orange oil

1 cup freshly shredded carrots
$\frac{1}{2}$ cup raisins

Pineapple Buttercream Frosting (page 137)

1. Position a rack in the center of the oven and preheat to 350° F. Lightly spray two 8-inch round nonstick cake pans with oil.

2. In a medium bowl, whisk the flour, baking soda, cinnamon, and salt until well combined. Set aside.

3. In another medium bowl, using a handheld electric mixer set at high speed, beat the drained pineapple, brown sugar, buttermilk, applesauce, egg, egg whites, oil, and orange zest until frothy, about 2 minutes. Make a well in the center of the dry ingredients, and pour in the buttermilk mixture. Using a spoon, stir just until moistened (there should be a few traces of flour remaining). Add the carrots and raisins and fold just until the flour is incorporated. Do not overmix. Divide the batter equally between the prepared pans. Using a gentle touch, smooth the tops.

4. Bake until the top of the cakes springs back when pressed gently in the center and the sides are pulling away from the pans, 25 to 30 minutes. Do not overbake. Cool in the pans on wire cake racks for 10 minutes. Unmold onto the racks, turn right side up, and cool completely.

5. Place one cake, flat side up, on a serving platter. Spread with about ¹/₂ cup frosting. Place the other layer, round side up, on the bottom layer. Frost the top of the cake with the remaining frosting and serve.

CARROT-PINEAPPLE SHEET CAKE: Position a rack in the center of the oven and preheat to 350° F. Lightly spray a 9 x 13-inch baking pan with oil. Make the batter according to the recipe instructions. Turn the batter into the prepared pan and gently smooth the top. Bake until the top of the cake springs back when lightly pressed in the center and the edges are beginning to pull away from the sides of the pan, about 25 minutes. Cool in the pan on a wire cake rack. If desired, sift 1 tablespoon confectioners' sugar over the top before serving. Makes 15 servings.

....

Nutritional Analyses

Carrot-Pineapple Layer Cake (with frosting, each serving): *About 353 calories (7 percent from protein; 84 percent from carbohydrates; 9 percent from fat), 7 grams protein, 76 grams carbohydrates, 4 grams fat (1 gram saturated fat), 22 milligrams cholesterol, 167 milligrams sodium*
Carrot-Pineapple Sheet Cake (unfrosted, each serving): *About 177 calories (9 percent from protein; 82 percent from carbohydrates; 9 percent from fat), 4 grams protein, 38 grams carbohydrates, 2 grams fat (less than 1 gram saturated fat), 15 milligrams cholesterol, 132 milligrams sodium*

Chocolate Fudge Layer Cake

MAKES 12 SERVINGS

· ❋ ·

New Creaming Method

Mom's Chocolate Fudge Cake recipe used whole eggs, sour cream, and two sticks of butter. I knew that if I just kept at it, I could come up with an equally great cake that I could serve to my family without pangs of guilt. Here is my version, in all of its deep, dark glory, my daughter Elizabeth's favorite. (Because of the cake's low fat content, it can be a little tricky—just follow the recipe exactly, and you'll be fine.)

Nonstick canola oil spray

2 ounces bittersweet or semisweet chocolate
1 ¾ cups sugar
4 tablespoons (½ stick) unsalted butter, at room
    temperature
½ cup low-fat buttermilk
1 large egg
2 large egg whites

2 cups cake flour, not self-rising (*spoon* into measuring
    cup and level top)
½ cup Dutch-process cocoa powder (*spoon* into
    measuring cup and level top)

2 teaspoons instant espresso powder
1 cup boiling water
1 teaspoon baking soda

Fudgy Chocolate Frosting (page 133)

1. Position a rack in the center of the oven and preheat to 350° F. Lightly spray two 8-inch round nonstick cake pans with oil. Line the bottoms of the pans with rounds of waxed paper and spray again.

2. Melt the chocolate according to the directions on pages 256–57. Let cool until tepid.

3. In a medium bowl, using a handheld electric mixer set at medium speed, beat the sugar and butter until the mixture resembles coarse bread crumbs, scraping down the sides of the cup with a rubber spatula, about 2 minutes. Beat in the melted chocolate. Add the buttermilk, egg, and egg whites and beat until smooth.

4. In a medium bowl, whisk the flour and cocoa until well combined. (If the cocoa is lumpy, sift it, after measuring, onto a piece of waxed paper). With a spoon, mix the flour mixture into the wet ingredients, scraping down the sides and bottom of the bowl with a rubber spatula. Mix until smooth. Dissolve the coffee in the boiling water. Hold the coffee mixture over the mixing bowl and add the baking soda, as the mixture may foam over. Add to the batter. Stir until smooth. The batter will be very thin. Divide it equally between the prepared pans.

5. Bake until the cakes begin to pull away from the sides of the pans, about 30 minutes. (You can't test this cake by pressing the center as it has a thin crisp top crust.) Do not overbake. Do not open the oven until the last 5 minutes of baking. Cool in the pans on wire cake racks for 10 minutes. Invert onto the racks and remove the waxed paper. Turn right side up and cool completely. Using a serrated cake knife, trim the top crusts off each cake layer.

6. Place one cake, flat side up, on a serving platter. Spread with about 1/2 cup frosting. Place the other layer, round side up, on the bottom layer. Frost the top of the cake with the remaining frosting and serve.

....

Nutritional Analysis
Each serving: *About 322 calories (5 percent from protein; 70 percent from carbohydrates; 24 percent from fat), 5 grams protein, 61 grams carbohydrates, 9 grams fat (5 grams saturated fat), 31 milligrams cholesterol, 100 milligrams sodium*

Ginger Spice Layer Cake

MAKES 12 SERVINGS

· ✴ ·

New Classic Method

A generous helping of molasses and brown sugar gives this cake an especially robust flavor, and crystallized ginger lends a peppery note. Zesty buttercream frosting, sparked with lime zest and juice, provides a bright counterpoint.

Nonstick canola oil spray

2 ¼ cups whole wheat *pastry* flour (*spoon* into
    measuring cup and level top)
1 ½ teaspoons baking soda
2 teaspoons minced crystallized ginger
1 teaspoon ground ginger
1 teaspoon ground allspice
½ teaspoon ground cinnamon
⅛ teaspoon salt

¾ cup unsweetened applesauce
¾ cup packed dark brown sugar
¾ cup 1 percent low-fat milk
½ cup unsulphured molasses
1 large egg
2 large egg whites
1 tablespoon canola oil

Lime Buttercream Frosting (page 137)

1. Position a rack in the center of the oven and preheat to 350° F. Lightly spray two 8-inch round nonstick cake pans with nonstick spray.

2. In a medium bowl, whisk the flour, baking soda, crystallized ginger, ground ginger, allspice, cinnamon, and salt until well combined. Set aside.

3. In another medium bowl, using a handheld electric mixer set at high speed, beat the applesauce, brown sugar, milk, molasses, egg, egg whites, and oil until frothy, about 2 minutes. Make a well in the center of the dry ingredients, and pour in the applesauce mixture. Using a spoon, stir just until combined. The batter will be somewhat thin. Do not overmix. Divide the batter equally between the prepared pans.

4. Bake until the top of the cakes springs back when pressed gently in the centers and the sides are pulling away from the pans, about 25 minutes. Do not overbake. Cool in the pans on wire cake racks for 10 minutes. Unmold onto the racks, turn right side up, and cool completely.

5. Place one cake, flat side up, on a serving platter. Spread with about 1/2 cup frosting. Place the other layer, round side up, on the bottom layer. Frost the top of the cake with the remaining icing and serve.

GINGER SPICE SHEET CAKE: Position a rack in the center of the oven and preheat to 350° F. Lightly spray a 9 × 13-inch baking pan with oil. Make the batter according to the recipe instructions. Turn the batter into the prepared pan and gently smooth the top. Bake until the top of the cake springs back when lightly pressed in the center and the edges are beginning to pull away from the sides of the pan, about 25 minutes. Cool completely in the pan on a wire cake rack. If desired, sift 1 tablespoon confectioners' sugar over the top before serving. Makes 15 servings.

Nutritional Analyses

Ginger Spice Layer Cake (with frosting, each serving): *About 343 calories (7 percent from protein; 84 percent from carbohydrates; 9 percent from fat), 6 grams protein, 74 grams carbohydrates, 4 grams fat (1 gram saturated fat), 22 milligrams cholesterol, 155 milligrams sodium*
Ginger Spice Sheet Cake (unfrosted, each serving): *About 171 calories (9 percent from protein; 82 percent from carbohydrates; 9 percent from fat), 4 grams protein, 36 grams carbohydrates, 2 grams fat (less than 1 gram saturated fat), 15 milligrams cholesterol, 123 milligrams sodium*

Fresh Mango-Pecan Layer Cake

MAKES 12 SERVINGS

· ✳ ·

New Classic Method

*M*ango, like other fruit purees, is a fine substitute for butter in many baked goods. Save this recipe for late spring when mangoes are in season and inexpensive. They should be very ripe.

Nonstick canola oil spray

2 ½ **cups whole wheat *pastry* flour (*spoon* into measuring cup and level top)**
1 ½ **teaspoons baking soda**
1 **teaspoon ground cinnamon**
⅛ **teaspoon salt**

¾ **cup mango puree (1 large ripe mango)**
¼ **cup unsweetened applesauce, plus more if needed**
1 **cup packed dark brown sugar**
½ **cup low-fat buttermilk**
1 **large egg**
2 **large egg whites**
1 **tablespoon canola oil**
Grated zest of 1 orange or ¼ **teaspoon pure orange oil**

⅓ **cup toasted, finely chopped pecans**

Orange Cream Cheese Frosting (page 134)

1. Position a rack in the center of the oven and preheat to 350° F. Lightly spray two 8-inch round nonstick cake pans with oil.

2. In a medium bowl, whisk the flour, baking soda, cinnamon, and salt until well combined. Set aside.

3. Place the mango on its side on a work surface. The flat pit runs horizontally through the center—the trick is to cut the mango flesh off the pit. Using a sharp knife, cut off the top third of the mango. Turn the mango onto its cut side, and cut off the other top third. Scoop the flesh out of the peel with a large metal spoon. Puree the mango flesh in a blender or food processor. Measure ³/₄ cup, adding applesauce as needed to make up the balance. (Pare the mango pit and nibble off the flesh as the cook's treat.)

4. In another medium bowl, using a handheld electric mixer set at high speed, beat the mango puree, brown sugar, additional ¹/₄ cup applesauce, buttermilk, egg, egg whites, oil, and orange zest until frothy, about 2 minutes. Make a well in the center of the dry ingredients, and pour in the mango mixture. Using a wooden spoon, stir just until moistened (there should be a few traces of flour remaining). Add the pecans and fold just until the flour is incorporated. Do not overmix. Divide the batter equally between the prepared pans. Using a gentle touch, smooth the tops.

5. Bake until the top of cakes springs back when pressed gently in the center and the sides are pulling away from the pans, 25 to 30 minutes. Do not overbake. Cool in the pans on wire cake racks for 10 minutes. Unmold onto the racks, turn right side up, and cool completely.

6. Place one cake, flat side up, on a serving platter. Spread with about ¹/₂ cup frosting. Place the other layer, round side up, on the bottom layer. Frost the top of the cake with the remaining icing. Serve. To store, cover and refrigerate the frosted cake.

FRESH MANGO-PECAN SHEET CAKE: Position a rack in the center of the oven and preheat to 350° F. Lightly spray a 9 × 13-inch baking pan with oil. Make the batter according to the recipe instructions. Turn the batter into the prepared pan and gently smooth the top. Bake until the top of the cake springs back when lightly pressed in the center and the edges are beginning to pull away from the sides of the pan, about 25 minutes. Cool completely in the pan on a wire cake rack. If desired, sift 1 tablespoon confectioners' sugar over the top before serving. Makes 15 servings.

....

Nutritional Analyses

Fresh Mango-Pecan Layer Cake (with frosting, each serving): *About 307 calories (9 percent from protein; 75 percent from carbohydrates; 16 percent from fat), 7 grams protein, 60 grams carbohydrates, 6 grams fat (less than 1 gram saturated fat), 23 milligrams cholesterol, 209 milligrams sodium*

Fresh Mango-Pecan Sheet Cake (unfrosted, each serving): *About 177 calories (9 percent calories from protein; 75 percent from carbohydrates; 16 percent from fat), 4 grams protein, 34 grams carbohydrates, 3 grams fat (less than 1 gram saturated fat), 15 milligrams cholesterol, 125 milligrams sodium*

Orange Sponge Cake with Fresh Berry Compote

· 🌟 ·

This classic cake has an elegant simplicity. My grandma Jenny made it for practically every occasion. Many sponge cake recipes use baking powder for leavening, but I prefer the original method that depends on the rise provided by the beaten eggs.

BERRY COMPOTE

> 2 cups sliced fresh strawberries
>
> 1 cup fresh raspberries
>
> 1 cup fresh blueberries or blackberries
>
> 2 tablespoons sugar
>
> 1 tablespoon fresh lemon or orange juice

ORANGE SPONGE CAKE

> 1 cup sugar
>
> 3 large egg yolks, at room temperature
>
> $\frac{1}{3}$ cup fresh orange juice or water
>
> Grated zest of 1 orange or $\frac{1}{4}$ teaspoon pure orange oil
>
> 1 cup cake flour, *not* self-rising (*spoon* into measuring cup and level top)
>
> 5 large egg whites, at room temperature (see page 253)
>
> $\frac{1}{8}$ teaspoon salt

> Confectioners' sugar, for sprinkling

1. To make the berry compote, combine the strawberries, raspberries, and blueberries in a medium bowl. Transfer 1 cup of the mixed berries with the sugar and lemon juice to a blender or food processor and puree. Stir the puree into the remaining berries. Cover and refrigerate until ready to serve.

2. Position a rack in the center of the oven and preheat to 325°F.

3. In a medium bowl, using a handheld electric mixer on high speed, beat the sugar, egg yolks, orange juice, and orange zest until thick and pale yellow, about 5 minutes.

4. Sift the flour over the beaten yolk mixture. Using a large rubber spatula, gently fold in the flour. Do not overmix.

5. Using very clean, dry beaters and a greasefree bowl, beat the egg whites on low speed until foamy. Add the salt and beat until soft peaks form. Stir a large spoonful of the egg whites into the yolk mixture. Fold in the remaining whites. Using a gentle touch, transfer the batter to an ungreased 10-inch tube pan, preferably *not* nonstick.

6. Bake until the cake is golden brown and the top springs back when pressed gently, 45 to 55 minutes. Invert the cake pan (if the cake pan doesn't have feet to keep the cake from touching the surface, invert the cake in pan on a standing bottle or funnel) and let stand until the cake is completely cooled. Using a metal spatula, carefully loosen the cake from the sides of the pan and place it on a serving platter.

7. Sprinkle with the confectioners' sugar. Slice and serve with the berry compote.

Nutritional Analyses

Orange Sponge Cake, with compote (each serving): *About 145 calories (8 percent from fat; 83 percent from carbohydrates; 9 percent from fat), 3 grams protein, 32 grams carbohydrates, 2 grams fat (less than 1 gram saturated fat), 53 milligrams cholesterol, 48 milligrams sodium*

Orange Sponge Cake, without compote (each serving): *About 118 calories (9 percent calories protein; 81 percent from carbohydrates; 9 percent from fat), 3 grams protein, 25 grams carbohydrates, 1 gram fat (less than 1 gram saturated fat), 53 milligrams cholesterol, 47 milligrams sodium*

Berry Compote (each serving): *About 27 calories (4 percent from protein; 90 percent from carbohydrates; 6 percent from fat), less than 1 gram protein, 7 grams carbohydrates, less than 1 gram fat (0 grams saturated fat), 0 milligrams cholesterol, 1 milligram sodium*

Autumn Pumpkin Layer Cake

MAKES 12 SERVINGS

• ❋ •

New Classic Method

The flavors of pumpkin and cranberry are as much a part of the autumn experience as colorful leaves and the scent of firewood. This cake would be welcome at a Thanksgiving buffet.

Nonstick canola oil spray

2 ½ cups whole wheat *pastry* flour (*spoon* into measuring cup and level top)

1 teaspoon baking soda

1 teaspoon ground cinnamon

½ teaspoon freshly grated nutmeg

⅛ teaspoon salt

¾ cup canned pumpkin

½ cup unsweetened applesauce

½ cup maple syrup, preferably grade B

Grated zest of 1 orange or ¼ teaspoon pure orange oil

½ cup fresh orange juice or water

3 large egg whites

1 tablespoon canola oil

1 tablespoon vanilla extract

½ cup coarsely chopped fresh or frozen (do not thaw) cranberries

Maple Buttercream Frosting (page 137)

1. Position a rack in the center of the oven and preheat to 350° F. Lightly spray two 8-inch round nonstick cake pans with oil.

2. In a medium bowl, whisk the flour, baking soda, cinnamon, nutmeg, and salt until well combined. Set aside.

3. In another medium bowl, using a handheld electric mixer set at high speed, beat the pumpkin, applesauce, maple syrup, orange zest and juice, egg whites, oil, and vanilla until lightened and frothy, about 2 minutes. Make a well in the center of the dry ingredients and pour in the pumpkin mixture. Using a spoon, stir just until combined. Fold in the cranberries. Do not overmix. Divide the batter equally between the prepared pans. Using a gentle touch, smooth the tops.

4. Bake until the top of the cakes springs back when pressed gently in the center and the sides are pulling away from the pans, 25 to 30 minutes. Do not overbake. Cool in the pans on wire cake racks for 10 minutes. Unmold onto the racks, turn right side up, and cool completely.

5. Place one cake, flat side up, on a serving platter. Spread with about ¹/₂ cup frosting. Place the other layer, round side up, on the bottom layer. Frost the top of the cake with the remaining icing. Serve.

Autumn Pumpkin Sheet Cake: Position a rack in the center of the oven and preheat to 350° F. Lightly spray a 9 × 13-inch baking pan with oil. Make the batter according to the recipe instructions. Turn the batter into the prepared pan and gently smooth the top. Bake until the top of the cake springs back when lightly pressed in the center and the edges of the cake are beginning to pull away from the sides of the pan, about 25 minutes. Cool completely in the pan on a wire cake rack. If desired, sift 1 tablespoon confectioners' sugar over the top before serving. Makes 15 servings.

Nutritional Analyses

Autumn Pumpkin Layer Cake (with frosting, each serving): *About 283 calories (8 percent from protein; 83 percent from carbohydrates; 10 percent from fat), 6 grams protein, 60 grams carbohydrates, 3 grams fat (1 gram saturated fat), 4 milligrams cholesterol, 121 milligrams sodium*

Autumn Pumpkin Sheet Cake (unfrosted, each serving): *About 132 calories (11 percent from protein; 81 percent from carbohydrates; 9 percent from fat), 4 grams protein, 28 grams carbohydrates, 1 gram fat (1 gram saturated fat), 0 milligrams cholesterol, 95 milligrams sodium*

Sarah's White Cake (or Cupcakes)

MAKES 12 SERVINGS OR CUPCAKES

· ※ ·

New Creaming Method

*A*n old-fashioned white layer cake is a favorite special-occasion dessert. My Healthy Oven customers kept asking me to come up with a reduced-fat version—and frankly, I wanted one for my own family, too. I used my mother's family recipe as a template, baking and adjusting it more than one hundred times (I counted) before I was satisfied with the results. It is even moister than the original! The timings are very exact. Just follow them and don't overmix the batter, and you'll have sweet success. Make these into cupcakes for a kids' birthday party and they'll love them.

Nonstick canola oil spray

2 cups cake flour, *not* self-rising (*spoon* into
   measuring cup and level top)
2 teaspoons baking powder
1/8 teaspoon salt

4 tablespoons (1/2 stick) unsalted butter, at
   room temperature
1 cup sugar

1 cup 1 percent milk
1 large egg
2 tablespoons instant nonfat dry milk powder
   (do not reconstitute)
1 teaspoon vanilla extract
1/4 teaspoon almond extract (optional)

Fudgy Chocolate Frosting (page 133)

1. Position a rack in the center of the oven and preheat to 350° F. Lightly spray an 8-inch round nonstick cake pan with oil.

2. In a medium bowl, whisk the flour, baking powder, and salt until well combined. Set aside.

3. In a medium bowl, using a handheld electric mixer set at high speed, beat the butter and sugar until the mixture resembles coarse bread crumbs, scraping down the sides of the bowl with a rubber spatula, about 1 1/2 minutes.

4. In a small bowl, beat the milk, egg, instant dry milk powder, vanilla, and almond extract, if using it, to combine. Pour into the butter/sugar mixture. Starting on low speed and increasing to high, beat until the mixture is frothy, about 1 minute.

5. Make a well in the center of the dry ingredients and pour in the milk mixture. Using a wooden spoon, stir just until the flour disappears. Using the electric mixer on high speed, beat just for 3 seconds. Do not overmix. Using a gentle touch, spread the batter evenly in the prepared pan.

6. Bake until the top of the cake springs back when pressed gently in the center and the sides are pulling away from the pan, about 30 minutes (do not open the oven until the cake has baked for at least 25 minutes). Do not overbake. Cool in the pan on a wire cake rack for 10 minutes. Unmold onto the rack, turn right side up, and cool completely.

7. Place the cooled cake on a serving platter. Spread with the frosting and serve.

SARAH'S WHITE CUPCAKES: Place paper cupcake liners in twelve 2 3/4 × 1 1/2-inch muffin cups. Spray the liners with nonstick canola oil spray. Divide the batter equally among the liners. Bake until the tops of the muffins are lightly browned and spring back when pressed in the center, about 20 minutes. Let cool in the pan on a wire cake rack for 10 minutes before removing from the cups. Cool completely on the rack. Serve. Makes 12 cupcakes.

....

Nutritional Analyses
Sarah's White Cake (with frosting, each serving or cupcake): *About 251 calories (5 percent from protein; 72 percent from carbohydrates; 23 percent from fat), 3 grams protein, 47 grams carbohydrates, 7 grams fat (4 grams saturated fat), 32 milligrams cholesterol, 99 milligrams sodium*
Sarah's White Cake (unfrosted, each serving or cupcake): *About 180 calories (6 percent from protein; 72 percent from carbohydrates; 22 percent from fat), 3 grams protein, 33 grams carbohydrates, 4 grams fat (3 grams saturated fat), 29 milligrams cholesterol, 97 milligrams sodium*

Zucchini-Currant Layer Cake

MAKES 12 SERVINGS

• ❋ •

New Class ic Method

Whenever I am stumped for what kind of layer cake to make, I pull out this recipe, and it's a crowd pleaser every time. Sometimes I mix zucchini and yellow crookneck squash—it looks terrific.

Nonstick canola oil spray

2 ½ cups whole wheat *pastry* flour (*spoon* into
    measuring cup and level top)
1 ½ teaspoons baking soda
1 teaspoon ground cinnamon
⅛ teaspoon salt

1 cup packed dark brown sugar
¾ cup unsweetened applesauce
¾ cup low-fat buttermilk
1 large egg
2 large egg whites
1 tablespoon canola oil
Grated zest of 1 orange or ¼ teaspoon pure orange oil

1 cup shredded zucchini
½ cup dried currants

Lemon Cream Cheese Frosting (page 135)

1. Position a rack in the center of the oven and preheat to 350° F. Lightly spray two 8-inch round nonstick cake pans with oil.

2. In a medium bowl, whisk the flour, baking soda, cinnamon, and salt until well combined. Set aside.

3. In another medium bowl, using a handheld electric mixer set at

high speed, beat the brown sugar, applesauce, buttermilk, egg, egg whites, oil, and orange zest until frothy, about 2 minutes. Make a well in the center of the dry ingredients and pour in the buttermilk mixture. Using a spoon, stir just until moistened (there should be a few traces of flour remaining). Add the zucchini and currants and fold just until the flour is incorporated. Do not overmix. Pour into the prepared pans. Using a gentle touch, smooth the tops.

4. Bake until the top of the cakes springs back when pressed gently in the center and the sides are pulling away from the pans, 25 to 30 minutes. Do not overbake. Cool in the pans on wire cake racks for 10 minutes. Unmold onto the racks, turn right side up, and cool completely.

5. Place one cake, flat side up, on a serving platter. Spread with about 1/2 cup frosting. Place the other layer, round side up, on the bottom layer. Frost the top of the cake with the remaining frosting and serve. To store, cover and refrigerate the frosted cake.

ZUCCHINI-CURRANT SHEET CAKE: Position a rack in the center of the oven and preheat to 350°F. Lightly spray a 9 × 13-inch baking pan with oil. Make the batter according to the recipe instructions. Turn the batter into the prepared pan and gently smooth the top. Bake until the top of the cake springs back when lightly pressed in the center and the edges are beginning to pull away from the sides of the pan, about 25 minutes. Cool completely in the pan on a wire cake rack. If desired, sift 1 tablespoon confectioners' sugar over the top before serving. Makes 15 servings.

Nutritional Analyses

Zucchini-Currant Layer Cake (with frosting, each serving): *About 299 calories (9 percent from protein; 80 percent from carbohydrates; 11 percent from fat), 7 grams protein, 62 grams carbohydrates, 4 grams fat (less than 1 gram saturated fat), 23 milligrams cholesterol, 215 milligrams sodium*

Zucchini-Currant Sheet Cake (unfrosted, each serving): *About 170 calories (10 percent from protein; 82 percent from carbohydrates; 9 percent from fat), 4 grams protein, 36 grams carbohydrates, 2 grams fat (less than 1 gram saturated fat), 15 milligrams cholesterol, 130 milligrams sodium*

Modern New York Cheesecake

MAKES 12 SERVINGS

· ✳ ·

*A*t a recent neighborhood party, this stopped the show. When I told them it was low-fat, I had them worried—they couldn't believe it. This cheesecake, which uses a meringue for its base, is so light and flavorful, and so attuned to today's tastes, that you may never serve clunky old-fashioned cheesecake again. My husband, Reed, could eat the whole cake if our kids didn't make him share. At a dinner party, I serve it with Strawberry Sauce (page 142).

Nonstick canola oil spray

GRAHAM CRACKER CRUST
1 ¼ cups graham cracker crumbs
¼ cup sugar
3 tablespoons unsalted butter, melted

CHEESECAKE
4 large egg whites, at room temperature (page 253)
1 cup sugar
12 ounces Neufchâtel cheese (do not use nonfat cream cheese), at room temperature and well softened
1 teaspoon vanilla extract

TOPPING
1 ½ cups reduced-fat sour cream
2 teaspoons sugar
½ teaspoon vanilla extract

1. Position a rack in the upper third of the oven and preheat to 350° F. Lightly spray a 9-inch nonstick springform pan with oil.

2. To make the crust, in a medium bowl, stir the cracker crumbs, sugar, and butter until well combined. Press the mixture evenly and firmly into the bottom of the prepared pan. Set the crust aside.

3. In a grease-free medium bowl, using a handheld electric mixer set at low speed, beat the egg whites until foamy. Increase the speed to high and beat until soft peaks begin to form. Gradually beat in the sugar until the mixture forms stiff, shiny peaks.

4. In another medium bowl, beat the cheese and vanilla on medium speed until smooth, scraping down the sides of the bowl as needed with a rubber spatula. Add the egg whites and beat on low speed until just combined. Do not overmix—it should take no longer than 10 seconds. Turn into the prepared pan and smooth the top.

5. Bake until the edges of the cake are slightly puffed and very lightly browned, about 25 minutes. The center will seem somewhat unset, but will firm when chilled. Remove the cake pan to a wire cake rack. Increase the oven temperature to 475° F.

6. To make the topping, mix the sour cream, sugar, and vanilla in a small bowl. When the oven temperature reaches 475° F, spread the topping over the hot cheesecake. Return the cake to the oven and cook just until the topping looks set around the edges, about 5 minutes. Cool to room temperature in the pan on a wire cake rack. Cover with plastic wrap and refrigerate until chilled, at least 4 hours or overnight.

7. Remove the sides of the cheesecake pan. Serve chilled. Cut the cheesecake with a sharp, thin knife dipped into hot water.

Nutritional Analysis

Per serving: *About 278 calories (9 percent from protein; 51 percent from carbohydrates; 40 percent from fat), 6 grams protein, 36 grams carbohydrates, 13 grams fat (6 grams saturated fat), 39 milligrams cholesterol, 257 milligrams sodium*

Lemon Cheesecake with Blueberry Topping

· ❋ ·

*E*veryone loves the combination of lemon and blueberries, but I sometimes make this with orange zest and juice and a blackberry topping. It isn't one of those big, thick cheesecakes that are so rich you can only eat a mouthful before you start feeling guilty—it's mouthwatering and light.

Nonstick canola oil spray

Graham Cracker Crust (page 126)

CHEESECAKE
4 large egg whites, at room temperature (see page 253)
1 cup sugar
12 ounces Neufchâtel cheese (do not use nonfat cream cheese), at room temperature and well softened
Grated zest of 2 lemons or generous ¼ teaspoon pure lemon oil
2 tablespoons fresh lemon juice

BLUEBERRY TOPPING
1 cup water
¼ cup sugar, or more to taste
2 tablespoons cornstarch
12 ounces (1 ½ cups) fresh or frozen blueberries

1. Position a rack in the upper third of the oven and preheat to 350° F. Lightly spray a 9-inch nonstick springform pan with oil.

2. Press the crust mixture evenly and firmly into the bottom of the prepared pan. Set the crust aside.

3. In a grease-free medium bowl, using a handheld electric mixer set at low speed, beat the egg whites until foamy. Increase the speed to high and beat until soft peaks begin to form. Gradually beat in the sugar until the mixture forms stiff, shiny peaks.

4. In another medium bowl, beat the cheese, grated lemon peel and lemon juice on medium speed until smooth, scraping down the sides of the bowl as needed with a rubber spatula. Add the egg whites and beat on low speed until just combined. Do not overmix—it should take no longer than 10 seconds. Turn into the prepared pan and smooth the top.

5. Bake until the edges of the cake are slightly puffed and very lightly browned, about 25 minutes. The center will seem somewhat unset, but will firm when chilled. Cool completely in the pan on a wire cake rack.

6. To make the topping, in a medium saucepan, whisk 1 cup water with the sugar and cornstarch until the cornstarch dissolves. Bring to a boil over medium heat, stirring often. Add the blueberries. (If using frozen blueberries, cook until thawed, about 1 minute.) Remove from the heat and let cool to warm.

7. Spread the topping over the cheesecake. Cover with plastic wrap and refrigerate until chilled, at least 4 hours or overnight.

8. Remove the sides of the cheesecake pan. Serve chilled. Cut the cheesecake with a sharp, thin knife dipped into hot water.

....

Nutritional Analysis
Per serving: *About 282 calories (8 percent from protein; 59 percent from carbohydrates; 34 percent from fat), 5 grams protein, 42 grams carbohydrates, 11 grams fat (6 grams saturated fat), 30 milligrams cholesterol, 212 milligrams sodium*

Dark Chocolate Cheesecake

MAKES 12 SERVINGS

• ❋ •

You'd have to look a long time to find a more richly flavored chocolate cheesecake, regardless of its fat gram count. When I want to make a believer out of those diehards who contend that reduced-fat desserts aren't as good as the old artery-cloggers, I serve this. It always puts an end to the argument.

Nonstick canola oil spray

CHOCOLATE CRUST
  1 ¼ cups chocolate graham cracker crumbs
  ¼ cup sugar
  3 tablespoons unsalted butter, melted

CHEESECAKE
  1 ounce bittersweet or semisweet chocolate
  4 large egg whites, at room temperature (see page 253)
  1 cup sugar
  ¼ cup Dutch-process cocoa powder
  1 teaspoon instant espresso coffee powder or
    2 teaspoons regular instant coffee powder
  1 teaspoon vanilla extract
  12 ounces Neufchâtel cheese (do not use nonfat cream
    cheese), at room temperature and well softened

1. Position a rack in the upper third of the oven and preheat to 350° F. Lightly spray a 9-inch nonstick springform pan with oil.

2. To make the crust, in a medium bowl, stir the cracker crumbs, sugar, and butter until well combined. Press the mixture evenly and firmly into the bottom of the prepared pan. Set the crust aside.

3. Melt the chocolate according to the directions on pages 256–57. Set it aside and let cool to tepid, but still liquid.

4. In a grease-free medium bowl, using a handheld electric mixer set at low speed, beat the egg whites until foamy. Increase the speed to high and beat until soft peaks begin to form. Gradually beat in the sugar until the mixture forms stiff, shiny peaks.

5. In another medium bowl, beat the cooled chocolate, cocoa, coffee powder, and vanilla on medium speed until combined. Add the cheese and beat, scraping down the sides of the bowl as needed with a rubber spatula, until smooth. Add the egg whites and beat on low speed until just combined. Do not overmix—it should take no longer than 10 seconds. Turn into the prepared pan and smooth the top.

6. Bake until the edges of the cake are slightly puffed and very lightly browned, about 25 minutes. The center will seem somewhat unset, but will firm when chilled. Cool to room temperature in the pan on a wire cake rack. Cover with plastic wrap and refrigerate until chilled, at least 4 hours or overnight.

7. Remove the sides of the cheesecake pan. Serve chilled. Cut the cheesecake with a sharp, thin knife dipped into hot water.

Nutritional Analysis
Per serving: *About 283 calories (8 percent from protein; 52 percent from carbohydrates; 40 percent from fat), 6 grams protein, 39 grams carbohydrates, 13 grams fat (6 grams saturated fat), 30 milligrams cholesterol, 255 milligrams sodium*

That's the Icing on the Cake

Special occasions call for frosted layer cakes, but even my reduced-fat frosting contains calories and fat. So, I make just enough to fill the center and frost the top of the cake. If you want to frost the sides, make a double batch of frosting. On the other hand, if you have an 8-inch single-layer cake that you think could use a little icing, make half a batch.

There are other occasions (kids' birthday parties, potluck suppers, school events, backyard barbecues, and the like) when I want a simple sheet cake to feed a crowd. I rarely frost these cakes—I just top them with a little confectioners' sugar, and serve them with fresh fruit. If you do frost them, keep in mind that each frosting is nutritionally analyzed separately (pages 133, 135, and 137) for twelve servings, but each sheet cake makes fifteen servings, so the count per serving will be slightly lower.

The following layer cakes can also be prepared as sheet cakes. I have given the instructions and nutritional information with each basic recipe.

Fudgy Chocolate Frosting

• ❋ •

A double whammy of cocoa and chocolate makes this frosting especially fudgy.

> 1 ounce bittersweet or semisweet chocolate
> 1 teaspoon instant espresso coffee powder
> 2 tablespoons boiling water
> 1 tablespoon unsalted butter, melted
> 1 tablespoon Dutch-process cocoa powder
> 1 1/2 cups confectioners' sugar
> 2 tablespoons 1 percent low-fat milk
> 1/2 teaspoon vanilla extract

1. Melt the chocolate according to the instructions on pages 256–57. Let cool until tepid.

2. In a medium bowl, dissolve the coffee powder in the boiling water. Add the melted chocolate, melted butter, cocoa, and vanilla and stir to make a paste. Add the confectioners' sugar. Using an electric handheld mixer set at low speed, beat until combined. One tablespoon at a time, beat in enough milk to make a creamy, spreadable frosting. Use immediately, or cover. The frosting can be prepared up to 1 day ahead. Let the chilled frosting stand at room temperature until spreadable.

....

Nutritional Analysis
Per tablespoon: *About 53 calories (2 percent from protein; 71 percent from carbohydrates; 27 percent from fat), less than 1 gram protein, 10 grams carbohydrates, 2 grams fat (1 gram saturated fat), 2 milligrams cholesterol, 2 milligrams sodium*

Orange Cream Cheese Frosting

MAKES ABOUT 1¼ CUPS; ENOUGH TO FILL AND FROST
THE TOP OF AN 8-INCH DOUBLE LAYER CAKE, THE TOP OF
ONE 9 × 13-INCH SHEET CAKE, OR 12 CUPCAKES

• ❋ •

Reduced-fat Neufchatel cheese is the beginning of a great frosting. It is sometimes labeled "light" or "reduced-fat cream cheese," but don't use nonfat. I use meringue powder to stabilize the frosting and to make it thick and creamy. Make it with orange or lemon to get the flavor that best matches your cake. Because this frosting has cream cheese, store frosted cakes in the refrigerator. *If you want to frost a single 8- or 9-inch layer cake, make half of this recipe.*

> 2 cups confectioners' sugar (more if needed)
> 4 ounces Neufchâtel cheese, chilled
> 2 tablespoons meringue powder (see Note)
> Grated zest of 1 orange or ¼ teaspoon pure orange oil
> ½ teaspoon vanilla extract
> 1 teaspoon 1 percent milk (optional—more if needed)

In a medium bowl, using a handheld electric mixer set at low speed, beat the confectioners' sugar, cheese, meringue powder, orange zest, and vanilla, until smooth. The mixture will be crumbly for 2 to 3 minutes at first, but it will smooth out as you continue mixing. Use immediately or cover. Best used just after mixing. The frosting can be prepared up to 1 day ahead. To soften, beat again with 1 teaspoon or more of 1 percent milk, for a few minutes until spreadable. Keep frosting thick.

Note: Do not reconstitute the meringue powder or substitute fresh egg whites. You may substitute dried egg white powder, if necessary, but it works better with the meringue powder.

LEMON CREAM CHEESE FROSTING: Substitute the zest of 1 lemon, or ¼ teaspoon pure lemon oil for the orange zest.

Nutritional Analyses

Orange Cream Cheese Frosting (per tablespoon): *About 53 calories (8 percent from protein; 76 percent from carbohydrates; 16 percent from fat), 1 gram protein, 11 grams carbohydrates, 1 gram fat (0 grams saturated fat), 3 milligrams cholesterol, 32 milligrams sodium*

Lemon Cream Cheese Frosting (per tablespoon): *About 53 calories (8 percent from protein; 76 percent from carbohydrates; 16 percent from fat), 1 gram protein, 10 grams carbohydrates, 1 gram fat (0 grams saturated fat), 3 milligrams cholesterol, 32 milligrams sodium*

Vanilla Buttercream Frosting

MAKES ABOUT 1 1/4 CUPS; ENOUGH TO FILL AND FROST
THE TOP OF AN 8-INCH DOUBLE-LAYER CAKE, THE TOP OF
ONE 9 × 13-INCH SHEET CAKE, OR 12 CUPCAKES

· ⁂ ·

You'll have a whole world of frostings with this in your repertoire. The basic recipe uses plain old vanilla and water, but you can see how different flavorings and liquids would work. It went through many versions before I finally hit on the right formula. You'll never miss the stick of butter in the old recipe. *You can make half a recipe for a single 8- or 9-inch layer cake.*

> 3 cups confectioners' sugar
> 3 tablespoons meringue powder (see Note)
> 1 1/2 tablespoons unsalted butter, at room temperature
> 1 tablespoon light corn syrup
> 1 teaspoon vanilla extract
> 4 tablespoons water, plus more as needed

In a medium bowl, using a handheld electric mixer set at low speed, beat the sugar, meringue powder, butter, corn syrup, and vanilla until combined. Gradually beat in enough water to make a thick, spreadable frosting. Use immediately, or cover. Best used just after mixing. The frosting can be prepared up to 1 day ahead. To soften, beat again with 1 teaspoon (or more) of water, for a few minutes until spreadable. Keep frosting thick.

Note: Do not reconstitute the meringue powder or substitute fresh egg whites. You may substitute dried egg white powder if necessary, but it works better with meringue powder.

APPLE BUTTERCREAM FROSTING: Substitute unsweetened apple juice concentrate (thawed, if frozen) for the water.

MAPLE BUTTERCREAM FROSTING: Substitute pure maple syrup for the corn syrup. Reduce the vanilla to $^1\!/_2$ teaspoon. Add $^1\!/_4$ teaspoon maple extract, if desired.

MOCHA BUTTERCREAM FROSTING: Add $^1\!/_4$ cup Dutch-process cocoa to the confectioners' sugar. Substitute 4 to 6 tablespoons strong, cooled brewed coffee for the water.

ORANGE, LEMON, OR LIME BUTTERCREAM FROSTING: Add the grated zest of 1 orange, lemon, or lime; substitute fresh orange, lemon, or lime juice for the water or $^1\!/_4$ teaspoon each of either pure orange, lemon or lime oil.

PINEAPPLE BUTTERCREAM FROSTING: Substitute pineapple juice for the water.

Nutritional Analyses

Vanilla Buttercream Frosting (per tablespoon): *About 72 calories (4 percent from protein; 86 percent from carbohydrates; 10 percent from fat), 1 gram protein, 16 grams carbohydrates, 1 gram fat (less than 1 gram saturated fat), 2 milligrams cholesterol, 1 milligram sodium*

Apple Buttercream Frosting (per tablespoon): *About 78 calories (4 percent from protein; 86 percent from carbohydrates; 10 percent from fat), 1 gram protein, 17 grams carbohydrates, 1 gram fat (less than 1 gram saturated fat), 2 milligrams cholesterol, 2 milligrams sodium*

Maple Buttercream Frosting (per tablespoon): *About 72 calories (4 percent from fat; 86 percent from carbohydrates; 11 percent from fat), 1 gram protein, 16 grams carbohydrates, 1 gram fat (less than 1 gram saturated fat), 2 milligrams cholesterol, 1 milligram sodium*

Mocha Buttercream Frosting (per tablespoon): *About 74 calories (5 percent from protein; 84 percent from carbohydrates; 11 percent from fat), 1 gram protein, 16 grams carbohydrates, 1 gram fat (less than 1 gram saturated fat), 2 milligrams cholesterol, 2 milligrams sodium*

Orange, Lemon, or Lime Buttercream Frosting (per tablespoon): *About 77 calories (4 percent from protein; 86 percent from carbohydrates; 10 percent from fat), 1 gram protein, 17 grams carbohydrates, 1 gram fat (less than 1 gram saturated fat), 2 milligrams cholesterol, 1 milligram sodium*

Pineapple Buttercream Frosting (per tablespoon): *About 79 calories (4 percent from protein; 86 percent from carbohydrates; 10 percent from fat), 1 gram protein, 17 grams carbohydrates, 1 gram fat (less than 1 gram saturated fat), 2 milligrams cholesterol, 1 milligram sodium*

New "Whipped Cream"

· ❋ ·

When you want a dollop of sweet, fluffy, whipped cream on your dessert, but aren't willing to dive into a bowl full of fat and calories, make this delicious deceiver. To my taste, it blows those imitation whipped cream toppings out of the water. This recipe has been around a long time and I updated it. It's based on one from the 1946 *Joy of Cooking* that used regular evaporated milk (probably because of wartime rationing), but I use skimmed evaporated milk to reduce the fat. Gelatin stabilizes the whipped cream so it won't deflate. Serve it within an hour of making.

1 teaspoon unflavored gelatin
2 teaspoons cold water
One 12-ounce can evaporated *skimmed* milk
¼ cup sugar
1 ½ teaspoons vanilla extract
½ teaspoon almond extract (optional)

1. In a small bowl, sprinkle the gelatin over the cold water and let stand until the gelatin absorbs the water, about 5 minutes. Meanwhile, in a medium saucepan over medium-low heat, scald the evaporated milk (see Note below). Remove from the heat and add the gelatin. Stir well until the gelatin is completely dissolved, at least 1 minute. Stir in the sugar, vanilla, and almond extract if using it, until the sugar dissolves.

2. Refrigerate, stirring occasionally, until chilled, about 1 ½ hours, place in a freezer for about 45 minutes, or place the bowl in a larger bowl of ice water, and let it stand, stirring often, until chilled.

3. Using a handheld electric mixer set at high speed, beat until the mixture is thick and fluffy. Use immediately, or refrigerate for no more than 1 hour. If the mixture separates, beat again until combined.

Note: To scald the evaporated milk, place it in a heavy-bottomed pan on low heat. Stir occasionally until the milk is just hot with steam and small bubbles appearing around the edge; do not boil. Remove from the heat.

Nutritional Analysis

Per ¼ cup: *About 43 calories (25 percent from protein; 74 percent from carbohydrates; 1 percent from fat), 3 grams protein, 8 grams carbohydrates, less than 1 gram fat (0 grams saturated fat), 1 gram cholesterol, 37 milligrams sodium*

Orange Glaze

• ✳ •

Sometimes you want a simple glaze to embellish your cake. I lean toward citrus-flavored glazes, as the sharpness of the fruit balances the sugar's sweetness. If you want to glaze a loaf-shaped cake, make only half a batch of the glaze.

1 cup confectioners' sugar
Grated zest of 1 orange or ¹/₄ teaspoon pure orange oil
2 to 3 tablespoons fresh orange juice

Place the confectioners' sugar and zest in a medium bowl. Stir in enough of the orange juice to make a smooth glaze. The consistency should be a little thicker than heavy cream. Use immediately.

LEMON GLAZE: Substitute the grated zest of 1 lemon or ¹/₄ teaspoon pure lemon oil and fresh lemon juice for the orange.

LIME GLAZE: Substitute the grated zest of 1 lime or ¹/₄ teaspoon pure lime oil and fresh lime juice for the orange.

Nutritional Analyses:
Orange Glaze (per tablespoon): *About 37 calories (0 percent from protein; 100 percent from carbohydrates; 0 percent from fat), less than 1 gram protein, 10 grams carbohydrates, less than 1 gram fat (0 grams saturated fat), 0 milligrams cholesterol, less than 1 milligram sodium*
Lemon or Lime Glaze (per tablespoon): *About 36 calories (0 percent from fat; 100 percent from carbohydrates; 0 percent from fat), 0 grams protein, 9 grams carbohydrates, 0 grams fat (0 grams saturated fat), 0 milligrams cholesterol, less than 1 milligram sodium*

Vanilla Custard Sauce

MAKES 6 SERVINGS (1 $\frac{1}{2}$ CUPS)

· ✳ ·

Served warm or chilled, this is a reduced-fat version of the classic dessert sauce crème anglaise. It is an easy way to dress up simple cakes like the Double Delicious Gingerbread (page 72).

1 $\frac{1}{2}$ cups 1 percent low-fat milk
3 tablespoons sugar
1 large egg
1 tablespoon cornstarch
1 teaspoon vanilla extract

1. In a small saucepan over medium heat, heat the milk and sugar until very hot, stirring occasionally to dissolve the sugar, about 2 minutes.

2. In a small, heavy-bottomed saucepan, whisk the egg and cornstarch until combined. Gradually whisk in the hot milk. Cook over medium-low heat, stirring constantly with a wooden spatula (be sure to reach the corners of the pan), until simmering. Remove from the heat, add the vanilla, and whisk briskly to dissolve any small lumps. Strain into a bowl. Serve warm, or let cool to room temperature, cover, and refrigerate until chilled. (The sauce can be prepared up to 1 day ahead.)

GINGER CUSTARD SAUCE: Substitute dark brown sugar for the sugar. Reduce the vanilla to $\frac{1}{2}$ teaspoon. Add 1 tablespoon minced crystallized ginger and $\frac{1}{4}$ teaspoon ground ginger to the sauce after straining.

....

Nutritional Analysis
Vanilla Custard Sauce (per $\frac{1}{4}$ cup): *About 68 calories (18 percent from protein; 62 percent from carbohydrates; 20 percent from fat), 3 grams protein, 10 grams carbohydrates, 1 gram fat (less than 1 gram saturated fat), 38 milligrams cholesterol, 41 milligrams sodium*
Ginger Custard Sauce (per $\frac{1}{4}$ cup): *About 75 calories (16 percent from protein; 66 percent from carbohydrates; 18 percent from fat), 3 grams protein, 12 grams carbohydrates, 1 gram fat (less than 1 gram saturated fat), 38 milligrams cholesterol, 43 milligrams sodium*

Strawberry Sauce

MAKES 12 SERVINGS (ABOUT 1½ CUPS)

· 💥 ·

*B*right red and bursting with berry flavor, this sauce can be used to dress up a slice of cheesecake or angel food cake.

> **1 pint fresh strawberries, stemmed and sliced, or 2 cups unsweetened frozen strawberries, thawed**
> **2 tablespoons sugar, plus more as needed**
> **1 tablespoon fresh lemon juice**

In a food processor fitted with the metal blade or in a blender, puree the strawberries, sugar, and lemon juice. Taste, and add more sugar as needed. Transfer to a bowl, cover, and refrigerate until ready to serve, or for up to 2 days.

RASPBERRY SAUCE: Substitute 2 cups fresh or frozen and thawed raspberries for the strawberries.

....

Nutritional Analyses

Strawberry Sauce (per serving): *About 15 calories (4 percent from protein; 91 percent from carbohydrates; 5 percent from fat), less than 1 gram protein, 4 grams carbohydrates, less than 1 gram fat (less than 1 gram saturated fat), 0 milligrams cholesterol, less than 1 milligram sodium*
Raspberry Sauce (per serving): *About 18 calories (4 percent from protein; 91 percent from carbohydrates; 5 percent from fat), less than 1 gram protein, 4 grams carbohydrates, less than 1 gram fat (0 grams saturated fat), 0 milligrams cholesterol, 0 milligrams sodium*

The New Pie Cupboard:
Pies, Tarts,
and Other Pastries

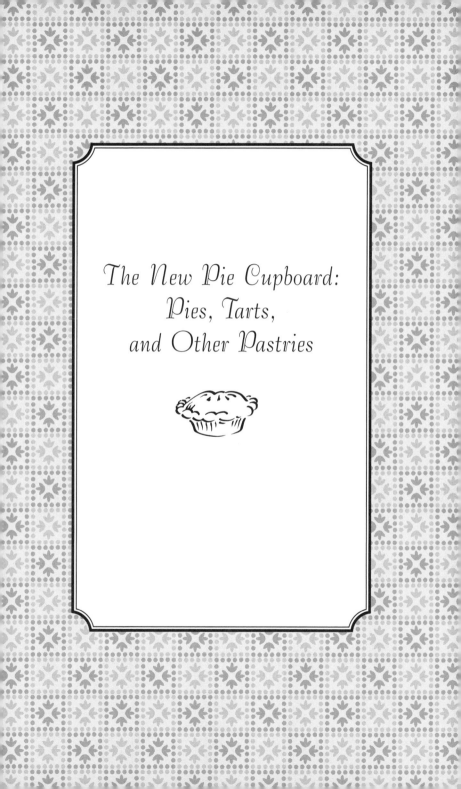

Perfect Pie Dough

MAKES 1 SINGLE-CRUST,
9-INCH ROUND PIE OR TART; 10 SERVINGS

· ❋ ·

*T*he perfect pie crust should be tender and buttery to create a delicious frame for the filling. Over the years, I tried to create a low-fat, old-fashioned pie crust, and I was never happy with the results. Finally, the answer came from my favorite professional baker, Nick Malgieri, author of *How to Bake*. Nick taught me how to make his wonderful dough which I adapted slightly, that has *just enough* butter to give it the pastry characteristics we all love—traditional doughs are usually overloaded with butter or vegetable shortening. It also includes a little baking powder for leavening and a splash of vinegar to help. I find it's best to shred the chilled butter so it is in small flakes, which are easier to cut into the flour.

Sweet with a cookie-like texture, this crust is not flaky, only tender and delicious. (Flaky pie crusts are made with vegetable shortening, which I do not like to use for health reasons.) The amount of sugar in the dough makes it a little sticky to work with (roll it out between two sheets of waxed paper to solve that problem). Also, the dough is best baked the day it is made. Freeze the rolled-out pie crust for 1 hour and it will hold its shape when baked blind without your having to line the shell with foil and weights (a procedure recommended by some bakers, but one that doesn't work well with this sweet, reduced-fat dough).

4 tablespoons (½ stick) unsalted butter, chilled
1 cup unbleached all-purpose flour (*spoon* into
    measuring cup and level top)
3 tablespoons sugar
¼ teaspoon baking powder
⅛ teaspoon salt
1 large egg yolk

144 · *The Healthy Oven Baking Book*

2 tablespoons ice water, plus more as needed
$\frac{1}{4}$ teaspoon cider vinegar or lemon juice

1. Using the large holes of a box grater, shred the chilled butter onto a plate. Freeze the shredded butter for 10 minutes.

2. In a medium mixing bowl, whisk the flour, sugar, baking powder,and salt to combine. Add the shredded butter. Using a pastry blender or two knives, cut in the butter until it resembles coarse cornmeal—no distinguishable pieces of butter should remain. (If you wish, use your fingertips to rub the butter into the flour mixture, but a pastry blender is much quicker. Be sure to use only your fingertips, and not your palms. The butter must stay cold, and warm palms may melt it.)

3. In another mixing bowl, thoroughly mix the egg yolk, ice water, and vinegar. Tossing the flour mixture with a fork, gradually stir in the liquid until the dough is thoroughly moistened but not wet, and clumps together. You may not need all of the liquid. To test the consistency, press the dough between your thumb and forefinger—it should hold together. If it won't, stir in additional ice water, 1 teaspoon at a time. Do not add so much liquid that the dough clumps into a solid ball—wet dough bakes into a tough pie crust. Gather the dough in the bowl to bring the clumps together. Gather it into a thick disk (the dough will remain somewhat crumbly), and wrap it in waxed paper (waxed paper works better than plastic wrap, which can make the exterior of the dough sticky). Refrigerate until chilled, at least 1 and up to 8 hours.

4. Prepare the pie pan by generously spraying with oil.

5. To roll out the dough, unwrap and place it on a piece of waxed paper. Beat the dough with the rolling pin to soften it slightly. Cover the dough with a second piece of waxed paper and roll it into a 12-inch round about $\frac{1}{8}$ inch thick. Work as quickly as possible so the dough doesn't get too warm. Patch and piece as necessary. Remove the top sheet of waxed paper. (If the dough sticks to the waxed paper, place the dough round on a baking sheet and freeze for 5 to 10 minutes until the waxed paper can be lifted off.)

6. Invert a prepared 9-inch ovenproof glass pie pan over the dough and quickly invert the pan and dough together, letting the excess dough hang over the sides of the pan. Gently press the dough snugly into the corners of the pan. (If the dough cracks, just press the cracks together. Gaps can be patched with a scrap of dough.) Peel off the waxed paper. For pies, fold the overhanging dough into the pan so the folded edge is flush with the edge of the pan or trim the excess dough for tarts. Prick the dough all over with the tines of a fork. Cover the pie crust with plastic wrap and freeze at least 1 hour or refrigerate overnight. The pie crust must be well chilled before baking. The pie crust can be frozen if well wrapped. Best used within a week.

Food Processor Pie Dough: If you wish, the flour and butter can be combined in a food processor, but mix the rest of the ingredients in a bowl. Food processors have strong motors, and it is very easy to overmix and toughen the dough. Place the flour, sugar, baking powder, and salt in a food processor fitted with the metal blade. Pulse three times to combine. Add the butter and pulse until the mixture resembles coarse meal. Transfer to a medium bowl, and proceed with step 3.

Nutritional Analysis
Per serving: *About 106 calories (6 percent from protein; 50 percent from carbohydrates; 44 percent from fat), 2 grams protein, 13 grams carbohydrates, 5 grams fat (3 grams saturated fat), 34 milligrams cholesterol, 37 milligrams sodium*

Apple Filo Tart

MAKES 8 SERVINGS

· 💥 ·

A lot of healthy cooks make pie crusts from filo dough, which makes a fine pastry under some, but not all, conditions. This recipe shows filo at its best, wrapping tender slices of sweet-tangy apples in thin, crispy layers of dough.

> **Nonstick canola oil spray**
>
> **FILLING**
> **2 large Golden Delicious apples, peeled,**
>   **cored, and cut lengthwise into $^{1}\!/_{2}$-inch slices**
> **2 tablespoons dark brown sugar**
> **1 teaspoon fresh lemon juice**
> **$^{1}\!/_{2}$ teaspoon ground cinnamon**
>
> **Eight 12 × 17-inch sheets filo dough,**
>   **thawed overnight (see Note)**

1. Position a rack in the center of the oven and preheat to 375° F. Lightly spray a nonstick baking sheet with oil. Set aside.

2. To make the filling, in a medium bowl, toss the apple slices, brown sugar, lemon juice, and cinnamon. Set aside.

3. Place 1 sheet of filo on a prepared nonstick baking sheet and very lightly spray it with oil. Top with the other filo sheets, lightly spraying each sheet with oil, and progressively arranging the sheets across each other at angles to form a "sunburst" pattern. Mound the apple filling in the center. Bring up the filo sheets to completely cover the filling. Spray the top of the filo with oil.

Note: For best results, thaw frozen filo dough overnight in the refrigerator. If thawed at room temperature, the sheets tend to stick together. Filo dough dries out quickly and can crack when exposed to air. Keep the stack of filo sheets covered with plastic wrap, and work quickly as the sheets are removed from the stack. Filo dough can be refrozen, as well.

4. Bake until the filo is deep golden brown, about 35 minutes. Cool on the baking sheet on a wire cake rack for 10 minutes. Slide the tart onto a serving platter. Serve warm.

Nutritional Analysis
Per serving: *About 104 calories (9 percent from protein; 88 percent from carbohydrates; 3 percent from fat), 2 grams protein, 24 grams carbohydrates, less than 1 gram fat (0 grams saturated fat), 0 milligrams cholesterol, 1 milligram sodium*

Classic French Apricot Tart

MAKES 10 SERVINGS

· ✳ ·

Pretty as a picture, this tart looks like something you'd admire in a French bakery window without all the fat. (French tart dough can have 8 tablespoons of butter to a cup of flour). Fresh apricots have a very short season in my area, so I use canned apricots, which work beautifully.

Nonstick canola oil spray

Perfect Pie Dough, made in advance (page 144)
Two 15 ¹/₂-ounce cans apricot halves in light syrup
¹/₂ cup apricot preserves (not all-fruit spread)
1 tablespoon sugar

1. Generously spray a 9 ¹/₂-inch tart pan with a removable bottom with oil. According to the instructions on pages 145–146, roll out the dough and transfer it to the prepared pan, fitting the dough snugly into the corners of the pan. Trim the excess dough to be flush with the edge of the pan. Cover with plastic wrap and freeze for 1 hour or refrigerate overnight.

2. Position a rack in the bottom third of the oven and place a baking sheet on the rack. Preheat the oven to 375° F. Place the tart pan on the hot baking sheet. Bake, checking occasionally to be sure the crust doesn't puff up (and piercing it with a fork if necessary to deflate the puff), until golden brown, about 20 minutes. Do not turn off oven.

3. Meanwhile, drain the apricots well, reserving 2 tablespoons of the syrup. Place the apricots, cut-sides down, on a double thickness of paper towels and let stand to remove as much moisture as possible.

4. In a small saucepan, bring the apricot preserves and reserved syrup to a boil over medium heat, stirring often. Reduce the heat to low and simmer for 2 minutes. Strain the glaze through a wire-mesh sieve into a small bowl and keep warm.

5. Remove the tart pan from the oven. Brush the inside of the crust with half the glaze. Place the drained apricots in the crust, cut sides down. Sprinkle with the sugar. Return to the oven and bake until the apricot juices are bubbling, about 20 minutes. Brush the apricots with the remaining glaze (if the glaze has cooled, reheat it over low heat.) Cool in the pan on a wire cake rack for 30 minutes. Remove the sides of the tart pan. Serve warm or cooled to room temperature. The tart is best served within 8 hours of baking.

Nutritional Analysis

Per serving: *About 195 calories (4 percent from protein; 73 percent from carbohydrates; 24 percent from fat), 2 grams protein, 37 grams carbohydrates, 5 grams fat (3 grams saturated fat), 34 milligrams cholesterol, 41 milligrams sodium*

Double Berry Icebox Pie

· ✳ ·

I'm sure a lot of moms out there have made strawberry pies like this, but with strawberry Jell-O. My version uses heaps of fresh strawberries, but the base for the filling is fresh raspberries. The pie will look so delicious you'll want to eat it right away, but avoid the temptation to cut it too soon—allow a full 2 hours for it to chill and set. If you wish, top each serving with a dollop of New "Whipped Cream" (page 138).

If you want a baked pie shell to use for your own fillings (maybe a low-fat chocolate pudding to make into a quick chocolate cream pie), follow these instructions through Step 3.

Perfect Pie Dough, made in advance (page 144)

FILLING

    1 envelope unflavored gelatin
    ¼ cup cold water
    2 cups fresh or frozen raspberries, thawed
    ⅓ cup sugar
    1 tablespoon fresh lemon juice
    2 pints fresh strawberries, hulled and halved
       (approximately 4 cups)

1. Generously spray a 9-inch ovenproof glass pie plate with oil. According to the directions on pages 145–46, roll out the pie dough and fit it into a prepared pan. Fold the excess dough flush with the edge of the pan. Cover with plastic wrap and freeze for 1 hour or refrigerate overnight.

2. Position a rack in the lower third of the oven and place a baking sheet on the rack. Preheat the oven to 375° F.

3. Place the pie pan on the hot baking sheet and bake, checking occasionally to be sure the crust doesn't puff up (and pricking the crust with a fork as necessary to deflate the puff), about 20 minutes. Remove the pie pan from the oven and cool completely on a wire cake rack.

4. To make the filling, in a small bowl, sprinkle the gelatin over the cold water. Set aside. In a food processor or blender, puree the raspberries. You should have 1 1/2 cups puree. In a small saucepan, bring the puree, sugar, and lemon juice to a boil over medium heat, stirring constantly. Remove from the heat and add the gelatin mixture. Stir until the gelatin is completely dissolved, at least 1 minute.

5. Place the raspberry sauce in a medium bowl set in a large bowl of ice water. Let it stand, stirring often, until chilled and syrupy, but not set, 10 to 20 minutes.

6. Arrange the strawberries in the cooled shell. Ladle the raspberry sauce over the strawberries. Refrigerate until set, at least 2 hours or overnight. Serve chilled.

Nutritional Analysis
Per serving: *About 162 calories (7 percent from protein; 64 percent from carbohydrates; 30 percent from fat), 3 grams protein, 27 grams carbohydrates, 6 grams fat (3 grams saturated fat), 34 milligrams cholesterol, 11 milligrams sodium*

Cherry-Cranberry Filo Rolls

MAKES 16 ROLLS

· ✺ ·

These are really mini-strudels with a chunky filling made from dried cherries and cranberries. You can use 1 cup of one or the other, but the combination is wonderful.

FILLING

    1 cup water
    ⅔ cup dried tart cherries
    ⅓ cup dried cranberries
    1 teaspoon quick-cooking tapioca
    ¼ teaspoon almond extract

    Sixteen 12 × 17-inch sheets filo dough, thawed
        overnight (see Note, page 149)
    Nonstick canola oil spray

    1 tablespoon sugar
    ½ teaspoon ground cinnamon

1. In a medium saucepan, combine the water, the dried cherries and cranberries, and the tapioca. Let stand for 5 minutes. Bring to a boil over medium heat, stirring often. Remove from the heat and stir in the almond extract. Let cool completely (the mixture will thicken as it cools).

2. Position a rack in the center of the oven and preheat to 375° F. Lightly spray a nonstick baking sheet with oil. Set aside. Stack four filo sheets on a work surface, arranging them with the long side facing you, and spraying each sheet lightly with oil. Using a pizza wheel or a sharp knife, cut the stack vertically into four strips each about 4¼-inches wide.

3. Working with one stacked strip at a time, spoon about 1 tablespoon of the cooled filling along the bottom, leaving a border 1 inch from the bottom and $\frac{1}{2}$ inch from each side. Starting from the bottom, roll up the filo strip to enclose the filling. Transfer it to a prepared baking sheet. Repeat with the remaining three strips, placing the rolls about 1 inch apart. Repeat the procedure with the other twelve sheets, stacking four sheets at a time. Spray the tops of the rolls with canola oil. In a small bowl, mix the sugar and cinnamon, and sprinkle the mixture over the tops of the rolls.

4. Bake until the rolls are crisp and golden brown, 10 to 15 minutes. Remove with a spatula to a wire cake rack to cool completely before serving.

Nutritional Analysis

Per serving: *About 94 calories (7 percent from protein; 92 percent from carbohydrates; 2 percent from fat), 2 grams protein, 30 grams carbohydrates, less than 1 gram fat (0 grams saturated fat), 0 milligrams cholesterol, less than 1 milligram sodium*

Lemon Meringue Tart

MAKES 10 SERVINGS

· ✳ ·

Lemon meringue pie is another all-American classic that I grew up on. This tart is a lightened version. The meringue uses three egg whites, so save the whites accumulated from separating the eggs for the yolks in the crust and lemon filling.

Nonstick canola oil spray

Perfect Pie Dough, made in advance (page 144)

LEMON FILLING
- $\frac{1}{2}$ cup sugar
- 2 tablespoons plus 1 teaspoon cornstarch
- 1 cup water
- 2 large egg yolks
- Grated zest of 2 lemons or generous $\frac{1}{4}$ teaspoon pure lemon oil
- $\frac{1}{3}$ cup fresh lemon juice

MERINGUE
- 3 large egg whites, at room temperature (see page 253)
- 3 tablespoons sugar

1. Generously spray a 9 $\frac{1}{2}$-inch tart pan with a removable bottom with oil. According to the directions on pages 145–46, roll out the pie dough and fit into the prepared tart pan, fitting the dough snugly into the corners of the pan. Trim the excess dough flush with the edges of the pan. Cover with plastic wrap and freeze for 1 hour or refrigerate overnight.

2. Position a rack in the center of the oven and place a baking sheet on the rack. Preheat to 375° F.

3. Place the tart pan on the hot baking sheet. Bake, checking occasionally to be sure the crust doesn't puff up (and pricking the crust with a fork as necessary to deflate the puff), until the crust is golden brown, about 20 minutes. Do not turn off the oven.

4. Meanwhile, make the filling. In a medium, heavy-bottomed saucepan, whisk the sugar and cornstarch. Gradually whisk in the water to dissolve the cornstarch. Whisk in the egg yolks. Stirring constantly with a wooden spatula (a wooden spatula works better than a spoon, as it will scrape the bottom of the pot more efficiently), being sure to reach into the corners of the saucepan, bring to a simmer over medium heat. The mixture will be very thick. Reduce the heat to low and simmer and stir for 30 seconds. Remove from the heat and stir in the lemon zest and lemon juice. Strain through a wire mesh strainer. Spread the hot filling into the pie crust.

5. Immediately make the meringue. In a large, grease-proof bowl, using a handheld electric mixer set on low, beat the egg whites until foamy. Increase the speed to high and beat until soft peaks form. Beat in the sugar, 1 tablespoon at a time, and beat until the whites are stiff and glossy. Spread the meringue over the hot filling, sealing it to the crust and using the back of a spoon to form decorative peaks.

6. Return the pie to the hot baking sheet in the oven. Bake until the meringue is golden brown, 10 to 15 minutes. Cool completely in the pan on a wire cake rack. Refrigerate, uncovered, until chilled, about 2 hours. Remove the sides from the tart pan. The pie is best served within 8 hours of baking.

Nutritional Analysis
Per serving: *About 188 calories (8 percent from protein; 63 percent from carbohydrates; 29 percent from fat), 4 grams protein, 30 grams carbohydrates, 6 grams fat (3 grams saturated fat), 76 milligrams cholesterol, 61 milligrams sodium*

Peach Galette

MAKES 10 SERVINGS

· ✳ ·

A galette is a free-form tart, baked without a pan, with the crust folded up around the filling. One of the best ways to make it is with peaches. Of course, fresh peaches are always wonderful, but when they are out of season, use canned peaches in juice, well drained. I have also used 3 ½ cups thawed frozen peach slices.

> 3 ripe fresh peaches or two 15-ounce cans peach slices
>   in juice, well drained and patted completely dry
>   with paper towels
> 2 tablespoons unbleached all-purpose flour
> 2 tablespoons sugar (optional, for fresh peaches only),
>   plus 1 teaspoon for sprinkling
> Perfect Pie Dough, made in advance (page 144)

1. If using fresh peaches, bring a medium saucepan of water to a boil over high heat. Add the peaches and boil until the skins are loosened, about 30 seconds. Drain and rinse under cold water until easy to handle. Cut the peaches into ½-inch-thick slices. In a medium bowl, toss the peaches with the flour and 2 tablespoons sugar, if using. Set aside.

2. Position a rack in the center of the oven and preheat to 375° F.

3. Place the dough between two sheets of waxed paper and roll it out into a 12-inch round about ⅛ inch thick. Peel off the top sheet of waxed paper (if the dough sticks, transfer it to a baking sheet and freeze until the waxed paper can be removed, 5 to 10 minutes).

4. Starting about 1 ½ inches from the edges of the dough, arrange overlapping peach slices in concentric circles. Carefully fold the dough up around the peaches, pleating it as necessary. Sprinkle the galette with the 1 teaspoon sugar. Lift the galette, still on the waxed paper, and place on a baking sheet. (If the dough seems soft and warm, place pan in freezer for 15 minutes or until well chilled. Place pan directly from the freezer into a hot oven.)

5. Bake until the crust is golden brown and the fruit is simmering, 30 minutes. Cool in the baking sheet on a wire cake rack for 10 minutes. Run a metal icing spatula under the galette to loosen, then slide it off the waxed paper onto a serving platter. Serve warm or cooled to room temperature.

Nutritional Analysis
Per serving: *About 133 calories (6 percent from protein; 59 percent from carbohydrates; 35 percent from fat), 2 grams protein, 20 grams carbohydrates, 5 grams fat (3 grams saturated fat), 34 milligrams cholesterol, 37 milligrams sodium*

Pear Baklava

MAKES 24 BAKLAVA

· ✴ ·

Of course, Greek pastries show off filo dough at its best. Instead of the typical nut filling, my baklava is stuffed with sautéed pears to make a delicious autumn dessert. You will have leftover filo dough scraps, which can be turned into an easy snack (my mom would never dream of tossing out regular pastry scraps, I couldn't bring myself to discard the filo strips, either).

FILLING

6 large Bosc pears, peeled, cored, and cut into
   $1/2$-inch cubes
$1/2$ cup sugar
1 tablespoon fresh lemon juice
1 teaspoon ground cinnamon

ASSEMBLY

Nonstick canola oil spray
One 16-ounce (12 × 17-inch sheets) box filo
   dough, thawed in refrigerator overnight
   (see Note, page 149)
3 tablespoons unsalted butter, melted or more,
   if needed
2 tablespoons finely chopped pecans

SYRUP

1 cup water
1 cup honey, preferably wildflower
$1/2$ cup sugar
1 tablespoon fresh lemon juice

1. To make the filling, in a large nonstick skillet, bring the pears, sugar, and lemon juice to a simmer over medium heat, stirring often. Cook, stirring occasionally, until the liquid evaporates and the pears are tender, 10 to 15 minutes. Remove from the heat, stir in the cinnamon, and let cool completely.

2. To assemble the baklava, position a rack in the center of the oven and preheat to 350° F. Lightly spray a 9 × 13-inch ovenproof glass baking pan with oil.

3. Place a stack of six filo sheets on a work surface. Put the pan on top of the filo, and use a sharp knife to trace around the pan and cut out 9 × 13-inch filo rectangles to fit the inside of the pan. Place one filo rectangle in the pan, and brush it very lightly with some of the melted butter. Repeat with the other five filo rectangles. Arrange half of the cooled pear filling over the filo (it will not cover it completely). Repeat the cutting and buttering procedure with six more filo sheets, placing them in the pan. Top with the remaining pear filling. Cut the remaining (approximately sixteen filo sheets, fit them into the pan, buttering each one. Brush the top of the baklava with butter, then sprinkle with the pecans.

4. Using a very sharp knife, score horizontally into three strips. Score vertically into four strips to make twelve rectangles. Score each rectangle diagonally to make twenty-four triangles. Bake until golden brown, 40 to 45 minutes. Transfer the pan to a wire cake rack.

5. To make the syrup, about 15 minutes before the baklava is done, combine 1 cup water, the honey, and the sugar in a medium saucepan. Bring to a boil over high heat, stirring often to dissolve the sugar. Reduce the heat to low and simmer for 5 minutes. Stir in the lemon juice and cook until slightly thickened, about 5 more minutes. Spoon the hot syrup over the hot baklava. Cool in the pan completely before serving.

CRISPY CINNAMON SNACKS: Cut leftover filo dough scraps lengthwise into strips about ¼ inch wide. Place in a large bowl. Spray lightly with canola oil spray. In a small bowl, mix 2 tablespoons sugar with ½ teaspoon ground cinnamon. Toss the cinnamon/sugar with the filo strips to coat. Spread on a nonstick cookie sheet. Bake in a preheated 350° F. oven until golden brown, about 10 minutes. Let cool and eat as a snack—they're great with sorbet. Makes 6 servings.

Nutritional Analyses

Pear Baklava (per serving): *About 172 calories (5 percent from protein; 84 percent from carbohydrates; 11 percent from fat), 2 grams protein, 38 grams carbohydrates, 2 grams fat (1 gram saturated fat), 4 milligrams cholesterol, 1 milligram sodium*

Crispy Cinnamon Sticks (per serving): *About 64 calories (10 percent from protein; 88 percent from carbohydrates; 2 percent from fat), 2 grams protein, 14 grams carbohydrates, less than 1 gram fat (0 grams saturated fat), 0 milligrams cholesterol, 0 milligrams sodium*

Thanksgiving Pumpkin Pie

MAKES 10 SERVINGS

· ❋ ·

Thanksgiving is the time for indulgence, and most healthy eaters would consider pumpkin pie one of those once-in-a-while luxuries. While this version uses evaporated skimmed milk, egg whites, and a lean pie crust, it has an old-fashioned flavor that will please even staunch traditionalists. It's based on a recipe from cooking teacher Gerri Weiner, who, in turn, uses her grandmother's original. Gerri makes her pies with freshly cooked winter squash, but I get excellent results from canned pumpkin without the extra trouble.

Perfect Pie Dough, made in advance (page 144)
One 15-ounce can pumpkin (1 ¼ cups)
One 12-ounce can evaporated skimmed milk
1 cup dark brown sugar
1 large egg
2 large egg whites
½ teaspoon ground ginger
¼ teaspoon ground cinnamon
¼ teaspoon freshly grated nutmeg

1. According to the instructions on pages 145–46, roll out the dough, fit it into a prepared 9-inch ovenproof glass pie pan, and fold the excess dough flush with the edge of the pan. Cover with plastic wrap and freeze for 1 hour or refrigerate overnight.

2. Position a rack in the bottom third of the oven and place a baking sheet on the rack. Preheat to 350° F.

3. In a medium bowl, stir the pumpkin, skimmed milk, brown sugar, egg, egg whites, ginger, cinnamon, and nutmeg until the sugar dissolves. Pour into the pie crust, and place the pan on the hot baking sheet in the oven.

4. Bake until the filling looks set (except for the very center, which will jiggle when the pie is shaken, but will firm up when chilled), about 1 hour. Cool to room temperature in the pan on a wire cake rack. Cover with plastic wrap and refrigerate until chilled, at least 2 hours or overnight. Serve chilled.

WINTER SQUASH PIE: Use 3 pounds Hubbard squash, sugar or cheese pumpkins (not the jack-o'-lantern variety), or butternut squash. Preheat the oven to 375° F. and line a baking sheet with aluminum foil. Cut the squash lengthwise and remove the seeds. Rub the cut surfaces of the squash with canola oil. Place, cut sides down, on the baking sheet. Bake until tender when pierced with a knife, 45 to 60 minutes. Let cool completely. Pare off the skins, or scoop the flesh out with a large spoon, discarding the skins. Puree the squash in a food processor. Place the squash puree in a paper towel–lined wire sieve set over a deep bowl. Let drain, stirring occasionally, until the puree is as thick as canned solid pack pumpkin, at least 1 hour. (The amount of drained excess liquid varies with the type of squash.) Substitute the squash puree for the canned pumpkin. Any leftover puree can be frozen and used just like canned pumpkin in baked recipes.

....

Nutritional Analysis
Thanksgiving Pumpkin Pie and Winter Squash Pie (per serving): *About 244 calories (10 percent from protein; 68 percent from carbohydrates; 22 percent from fat), 6 grams protein, 43 grams carbohydrates, 6 grams fat (3 grams saturated fat), 57 milligrams cholesterol, 107 milligrams sodium*

Old-Fashioned Raisin Pie

MAKES 10 SERVINGS

· ❄ ·

Sour cream raisin pie is an old farmhouse recipe that I have made lighter by substituting nonfat yogurt for the sour cream. The combination of tangy yogurt and sweet raisins is a winner.

Perfect Pie Dough, made in advance (page 144)

FILLING

> 1 large egg
> 3 large egg whites
> $\frac{1}{3}$ cup packed dark brown sugar
> 1 tablespoon plus 1 teaspoon cornstarch
> 2 teaspoons vanilla extract
> $\frac{1}{4}$ teaspoon ground cinnamon
> 1 $\frac{1}{2}$ cups plain nonfat yogurt
> 1 cup raisins

1. According to the instructions on pages 145–46, roll out the dough, fit it into a prepared 9-inch ovenproof glass pie pan, and fold the excess dough flush with the edge of the pan. Cover with plastic wrap and freeze for 1 hour or refrigerate overnight.

2. Position a rack in the bottom third of the oven and place a baking sheet on the rack. Preheat the oven to 400° F.

3. In a medium bowl, whisk the egg, egg whites, brown sugar, cornstarch, vanilla, and cinnamon until combined. Whisk in the yogurt, then the raisins. Pour into the crust. Place on the hot baking sheet in the oven.

4. Bake for 10 minutes. Reduce the oven temperature to 350° F, and bake until the edges of the custard are golden brown, 35 to 40 minutes. Cool to room temperature in the pan on a wire cake rack. Cover with

plastic wrap and refrigerate until chilled, at least 2 hours or overnight.
Serve chilled.

Nutritional Analysis

Per serving: *About 215 calories (10 percent from protein; 65 percent from carbohydrates;*
24 percent from fat), 6 grams protein, 36 grams carbohydrates, 6 grams fat (3 grams saturated fat),
56 milligrams cholesterol, 89 milligrams sodium

Raspberry Tart with Cornmeal Crust

MAKES 10 SERVINGS

· ✳ ·

W e have countless wild raspberry bushes in our backyard, and my kids are champion berry pickers. This is one of my favorite ways to use the harvest. The golden, sweet cornmeal crust is a perfect base for the tangy filling. The tart is also good with blueberries instead of raspberries.

FILLING

> 1 cup water
> 2 tablespoons sugar
> 2 tablespoons cornstarch
> 2 cups fresh or frozen raspberries

CRUST

> 1 cup unbleached all-purpose flour (*spoon* into measuring cup and level top)
> $\frac{1}{2}$ cup yellow cornmeal, preferably stone-ground
> $\frac{1}{2}$ cup sugar
> $\frac{1}{2}$ teaspoon baking powder
> Pinch of salt
> 2 tablespoons unsalted butter, chilled
>
> 1 large egg yolk
> 3 tablespoons ice water
>
> Nonstick canola oil spray

1. Using the large holes of a box grater, shred the chilled butter onto a plate and freeze for 10 minutes.

2. To make the crust, in a medium bowl, whisk the flour, cornmeal, sugar, baking powder, and salt until well combined. Using a pastry blender or your fingertips, cut the butter until the mixture resembles coarse bread crumbs. In a small bowl, mix the yolk and ice water. Tossing the flour mixture with a fork, gradually stir in the liquid until the dough is thoroughly moistened but not wet. The dough may not look moist, but will hold together when pressed between your thumb and forefinger. You may not need all of the egg/water mixture. Gather the dough in the bowl to bring the dough together (the dough will remain somewhat crumbly). Gather it into a thick disk and wrap it in waxed paper (waxed paper works better than plastic wrap, which can make the exterior of the dough sticky). Refrigerate until well chilled, about 1 hour.

3. Meanwhile, make the filling in a medium saucepan, whisk the water with the sugar and cornstarch until the cornstarch dissolves. Cook over medium heat, about 3 minutes, stirring occasionally, until simmering and thickened. Stir in the raspberries and immediately remove from the heat. (If using frozen raspberries, cook until thawed about 1 minute.) Cool completely.

4. Position a rack in the center of the oven and place a baking sheet on the rack. Preheat the oven to 350° F. Generously spray a 9 1/2-inch tart pan with a removable bottom with oil.

5. Place the dough between two sheets of waxed paper. Roll it out 1/8-inch thick. If the dough crumbles, just press it together. Place on baking sheet and freeze until it is very cold and the top sheet of waxed paper pulls away easily, 10 to 15 minutes. Set the tart pan bottom onto the center of the dough. Position the tart ring over the bottom. The dough should measure 2 inches larger than the tart pan bottom on all sides. Flip the cornmeal crust and tart pan over so the crust is in the pan, gently pressing the dough to fit the corners of the pan pressing any cracks together. Trim the excess dough flush with the edges of the pan. Pour the cooled raspberry filling into the crust.

6. Place the tart pan on the baking sheet in the oven. Bake until the crust is brown and the filling is simmering about 45 minutes. Lightly spray a piece of plastic wrap with canola oil spray. Place the sprayed side directly on the surface of the filling and poke a few holes in the wrap with a knife to allow the steam to escape. The steam helps soften the fill-

ing surface. Cool completely in the pan on a wire cake rack. Remove the sides of the pan and the plastic wrap and serve at room temperature.

Nutritional Analysis
Per serving: *About 156 calories (6 percent from protein; 79 percent from carbohydrates; 15 percent from fat), 2 grams protein, 31 grams carbohydrates, 3 grams fat (1 gram saturated fat), 27 milligrams cholesterol, 44 milligrams sodium*

Sweet Potato Cheesecake Pie

MAKES 10 SERVINGS

· ❄ ·

*H*ere's another offering for the holiday dessert table. Sweet potato pie is a favorite with Southern cooks. This is an unusual version made with yogurt cheese, which gives it a cheesecake-like consistency, and a graham cracker crust. Sweet potatoes are a good source of betacarotene. Use the orange-fleshed sweet potatoes, sometimes called yams.

Nonstick canola oil spray

GRAHAM CRACKER CRUST (see page 126)

FILLING

1 cup mashed sweet potatoes (see Note)

2 cups nonfat yogurt cheese, made in advance
(page 251)

$1/3$ cup plus 1 tablespoon packed dark brown sugar

$1/3$ cup instant nonfat dry milk powder (do not
reconstitute)

1 large egg

2 large egg whites

2 tablespoons cornstarch

Grated zest of 1 orange or $1/4$ teaspoon pure orange oil

1 teaspoon ground cinnamon

$1/4$ teaspoon ground ginger

$1/4$ teaspoon freshly grated nutmeg, for garnish

1. Position a rack in the center of the oven and preheat to 350° F. Spray a 9-inch ovenproof glass pie pan with oil.

2. Press the crust mixture firmly and evenly into the bottom and sides of the prepared pan. Fold the excess dough flush with the edge of the pan. Bake the crust until beginning to set, 8 to 10 minutes. Transfer to a wire cake rack and set aside to cool. Reduce the oven temperature to 325° F.

3. To make the filling, in a large bowl, using a handheld electric mixer set at medium speed, beat the mashed sweet potatoes with the yogurt cheese, brown sugar, dry milk powder, egg, egg whites, cornstarch, orange zest or oil, if using it, the cinnamon, and the ginger. Pour into the crust and smooth the top. Sprinkle with the nutmeg.

N o t e : To cook the sweet potatoes for the filling, place 2 medium orange-fleshed sweet potatoes (yams) in a large saucepan and cover with lightly salted cold water. Bring to a boil over high heat. Reduce the heat to medium and cook until the sweet potatoes are tender when pierced with the tip of a sharp knife, about 30 minutes. Drain and rinse under cold water until easy to handle. Peel and mash the sweet potatoes.

4. Bake until the edges of the filling are slightly puffed and lightly browned, about 30 minutes. Do not overbake—the center will seem unset but will firm when chilled. Cool to room temperature in the pan on the wire cake rack. Cover with plastic wrap and refrigerate until chilled, at least 4 hours or overnight. Serve chilled.

Nutritional Analysis
Per serving: *About 259 calories (14 percent from protein; 66 percent from carbohydrates; 19 percent from fat), 9 grams protein, 43 grams carbohydrates, 6 grams fat (3 grams saturated fat), 33 milligrams cholesterol, 198 milligrams sodium*

From the Cookie Jar: Bars, Cookies, and Brownies

Apple-Raisin Bars

MAKES 12 BARS

· ✺ ·

New Classic Method

These turn out moist and spicy—just the thing for a kid's lunch box. Slice the apple thinly so it is easy to cut when dividing into bars. If you like a chewier bar, substitute prune baby food for the applesauce.

Nonstick canola oil spray

1 $^1/_4$ cups whole wheat *pastry* flour (*spoon* into
    measuring cup and level top)
1 teaspoon ground cinnamon
$^1/_2$ teaspoon baking soda
$^1/_8$ teaspoon salt

$^2/_3$ cup unsweetened applesauce
$^1/_3$ cup packed dark brown sugar
2 tablespoons canola oil
1 large egg

1 Granny Smith apple, peeled, cored, and thinly sliced
    (about 1 $^1/_2$ cups)
$^1/_2$ cup raisins

1. Position a rack in the center of the oven and preheat to 350° F. Lightly spray an 11 × 7-inch nonstick baking pan with oil.

2. In a medium bowl, whisk the pastry flour, cinnamon, baking soda, and salt until well combined. Set aside.

3. In another medium bowl, using a handheld electric mixer set at high speed, beat the applesauce, sugar, oil, and egg until light in color and frothy, about 2 minutes. Make a well in the center of the dry ingredients, and pour in the applesauce mixture. Using a spoon, mix just until moistened (there should be a few wisps of flour remaining). Do not overmix.

Gently fold in the apple and raisins until the flour is incorporated. Using a light touch, spread the batter into the prepared pan.

4. Bake until the sides pull away from the pan and the top springs back when gently pressed in the center, 25 to 30 minutes. Do not overbake. Cool completely in the pan on a wire cake rack. Cut into twelve equal bars.

Nutritional Analysis

Per bar: *About 125 calories (7 percent from protein; 72 percent from carbohydrates; 20 percent from fat), 2 grams protein, 24 grams carbohydrates, 3 grams fat (less than 1 gram saturated fat), 18 milligrams cholesterol, 65 milligrams sodium*

Chunky Banana Bars

MAKES 12 BARS

· ❋ ·

Method: New Classic

The ultimate snack cookie? It'll remind you of a banana cake, but packed with coconut, raisins, cranberries, and chocolate chips. Add some nuts, too, if you like.

Nonstick canola oil spray

2 ¹/₂ cups whole wheat *pastry* flour (*spoon* into
    measuring cup and level top)
1 teaspoon baking powder
1 teaspoon ground cinnamon
¹/₈ teaspoon salt

1 cup mashed ripe bananas (2 large)
¹/₂ cup sugar
¹/₂ cup unsweetened applesauce
¹/₂ cup apple juice or water
3 large egg whites
1 tablespoon canola oil
1 tablespoon vanilla extract

¹/₂ cup raisins
¹/₂ cup fresh or frozen (do not thaw) cranberries, or
    dried cranberries
¹/₂ cup sweetened shredded coconut flakes
¹/₄ cup semisweet chocolate chips

1. Position a rack in the center of the oven and preheat to 350° F. Lightly spray an 11 × 7-inch nonstick baking pan with oil.

2. In a medium bowl, whisk the flour, baking powder, cinnamon, and salt until well combined. Set aside.

3. In another medium bowl, using a handheld electric mixer set at high speed, beat the bananas, sugar, applesauce, apple juice, egg whites, oil, and vanilla until light in color and frothy. Make a well in the center of the dry ingredients and pour in the banana mixture. Using a spoon, stir just until moistened (there should be a few wisps of flour remaining). Add the raisins, cranberries, coconut, and chocolate chips and stir just until the batter is smooth. Do not overmix. Using a gentle touch, spread the batter in the prepared pan.

4. Bake until the top springs back when pressed gently in the center and the sides are pulling away from the pan, about 30 minutes. Do not overbake. Cool completely in the pan on a wire cake rack. Cut into twelve equal bars.

....

Nutritional Analysis
Per bar: *About 218 calories (9 percent from protein; 77 percent from carbohydrates; 15 percent from fat), 5 grams protein, 44 grams carbohydrates, 4 grams fat (1 gram saturated fat), 0 milligrams cholesterol, 66 milligrams sodium*

Vanilla Biscotti

· ❋ ·

New Classic Method

Biscotti are the new darlings of cookie lovers. They are the crispiest cookies of all, and always dipped into a cup of coffee, tea, or wine to soften before nibbling. Many old-country Italian recipes are naturally low in fat. Here's a basic recipe with lots of variations.

Nonstick canola oil spray

2 cups unbleached all-purpose flour (*spoon* into
    measuring cup and level top)
1 teaspoon baking powder
$\frac{1}{8}$ teaspoon salt

1 cup sugar
1 large egg
2 large egg whites
1 tablespoon canola oil
1 teaspoon vanilla extract

1. Position a rack in the center of the oven and preheat to 350° F. Lightly spray a nonstick baking sheet (preferably insulated), with oil.

2. In a medium bowl, whisk the flour, baking powder, and salt until well combined. Set aside.

3. In another medium bowl, using a handheld electric mixer set at high speed, beat the sugar, egg, egg whites, oil, and vanilla until frothy, about 2 minutes. Make a well in the center of the dry ingredients and pour in the egg mixture. Using a spoon, stir just until moistened. The dough will seem a little dry. Knead the dough briefly in the bowl just until it comes together. Shape the dough into two 7 × 2-inch logs on the baking sheet, spacing the logs about 1 inch apart.

4. Bake until the logs are golden brown and covered with tiny cracks, about 30 minutes. Remove the logs but do not turn off the oven. Transfer the logs to a wire cake rack and let them cool in the pan for 10 minutes. On a work surface, using a serrated knife, cut the logs on a slight diagonal into $3/8$-inch-thick slices. Return the slices to the baking sheet.

5. Bake for 10 minutes. Turn the biscotti over and continue baking until the edges are crisp, about 10 minutes more. The edges will not be very brown and the centers will be soft, but the biscotti will crisp when cooled. Do not overbake. Transfer to a wire cake rack and cool completely.

CHOCOLATE-COVERED BISCOTTI: Melt $1/2$ cup semisweet mini-chocolate chips according to the instructions on pages 256–57. Using a small metal spatula, spread the melted chocolate onto the cooled biscotti. Let stand to set the chocolate.

CHOCOLATE CHIP BISCOTTI: Add $1/2$ cup semisweet mini-chocolate chips to the dry ingredients.

LEMON-CRANBERRY BISCOTTI: Reduce the vanilla to $1/2$ teaspoon. Add $1/2$ cup dried cranberries to the dry ingredients, and the grated zest of 1 lemon or $1/4$ teaspoon pure lemon oil to the liquid ingredients.

MOCHA CHIP BISCOTTI: Substitute $1/4$ cup Dutch-process cocoa powder for an equal amount of the flour. Substitute 1 teaspoon baking soda for the baking powder. Add $1/2$ cup semisweet mini-chocolate chips to the dry ingredients and 1 teaspoon instant espresso powder to the liquid ingredients.

ORANGE-PECAN BISCOTTI: Add $1/2$ cup coarsely chopped pecans to the dry ingredients, and the zest of 1 orange or $1/4$ teaspoon pure orange oil to the liquid ingredients.

Nutritional Analyses

Vanilla Biscotti (per biscotti): *About 52 calories (8 percent from protein; 82 percent from carbohydrates; 10 percent from fat), 1 gram protein, 11 grams carbohydrates, less than 1 gram fat (0 grams saturated fat), 6 milligrams cholesterol, 22 milligrams sodium*

Chocolate-Covered Biscotti (per biscotti): *About 63 calories (7 percent from protein; 75 percent from carbohydrates; 17 percent from fat), 1 gram protein, 12 grams carbohydrates, 1 gram fat (0 grams saturated fat), 6 milligrams cholesterol, 22 milligrams sodium*

Chocolate Chip Biscotti (per biscotti): *About 63 calories (7 percent from protein; 75 percent from carbohydrates; 17 percent from fat), 1 gram protein, 12 grams carbohydrates, 1 gram fat (0 grams saturated fat), 6 milligrams cholesterol, 22 milligrams sodium*

Lemon-Cranberry Biscotti (per biscotti): *About 57 calories (8 percent from protein; 83 percent from carbohydrates; 9 percent from fat), 1 gram protein, 12 grams carbohydrates, less than 1 gram fat (0 grams saturated fat), 6 milligrams cholesterol, 22 milligrams sodium*

Mocha Chip Biscotti (per biscotti): *About 61 calories (8 percent from protein; 74 percent from carbohydrates; 18 percent from fat), 1 gram protein, 12 grams carbohydrates, 1 gram fat (0 grams saturated fat), 6 milligrams cholesterol, 36 milligrams sodium*

Orange-Pecan Biscotti (per biscotti): *About 62 calories (8 percent from protein; 70 percent from carbohydrates; 23 percent from fat), 1 gram protein, 11 grams carbohydrates, 1 gram fat (0 grams saturated fat), 6 milligrams cholesterol, 22 milligrams sodium*

Coconut Oatmeal Macaroons

MAKES ABOUT 32 COOKIES

• ❋ •

runchy on the outside and chewy within, macaroons are a real treat. Oatmeal gives these a delicious difference. It's a great recipe for using baking parchment paper, if you have it, because all macaroons tend to stick a little bit, even to nonstick cookie sheets.

Nonstick canola oil spray (optional, see Step 1)

4 large egg whites
²/₃ cup sugar
¹/₂ teaspoon vanilla extract
¹/₂ teaspoon almond extract
1 cup sweetened flaked coconut
¹/₂ cup quick-cooking oatmeal
¹/₂ cup whole wheat *pastry* flour (*spoon* into measuring cup and level top)
¹/₈ teaspoon salt

1. Position a rack in the center of the oven and preheat to 325° F. Lightly spray a large nonstick cookie sheet (preferably insulated) with oil, or line the sheet with parchment or waxed paper and spray again.

2. In a medium bowl, whisk the egg whites, sugar, vanilla, and almond extract until frothy. Stir in the coconut, oatmeal, flour, and salt. Drop heaping teaspoons of the dough about 1 inch apart onto the prepared baking sheet.

3. Bake until the cookies are golden brown, 20 to 25 minutes. Transfer the pan to a wire cake rack and cool completely.

Nutritional Analysis:
Per cookie: *About 42 calories (9 percent from protein; 71 percent from carbohydrates; 19 percent from fat), 1 gram protein, 8 grams carbohydrates, 1 gram fat (less than 1 gram saturated fat), 0 milligrams cholesterol, 17 milligrams sodium*

Fudge Brownies

MAKES 12 BROWNIES

· ✳ ·

*I*f you love fudgy, gooey, intensely chocolate brownies, but not the fat, try this blue ribbon recipe. I have reduced the fat in my mom's recipe by half, which is as low as I could go to keep its great taste and texture. These brownies are my son Zach's favorite.

Nonstick canola oil spray

4 tablespoons unsalted butter, melted and
    cooled to tepid

2 ounces bittersweet or semisweet chocolate

$^1/_2$ cup unbleached all-purpose flour (*spoon* into
    measuring cup and level top)
$^1/_3$ cup Dutch-process cocoa powder (*spoon* into
    measuring cup and level top)
$^1/_2$ teaspoon baking powder
$^1/_8$ teaspoon salt

1 cup sugar
1 large egg
2 large egg whites
1 tablespoon canola oil
2 teaspoons vanilla extract
1 teaspoon instant espresso powder

1. Position a rack in the center of the oven and preheat to 350° F. Lightly spray an 8-inch square nonstick baking pan with oil.

2. Melt the chocolate according to the instructions on pages 256–57. Let cool until tepid.

3. In a medium bowl, whisk the flour, cocoa, baking powder, and salt until well combined. If the cocoa is lumpy, sift it. Set aside.

4. Add the melted butter, sugar, egg, egg whites, oil, vanilla, and espresso powder to the chocolate mixture and whisk until smooth. Using a spoon, stir in the cocoa mixture. Scrape into the prepared pan and smooth the top.

5. Bake until the edges begin to pull away from the sides of the pan, for *exactly* 25 minutes. Do not overbake. The center will seem unset, but will firm when cooled. Cool completely in the pan on a wire cake rack. To serve, cut into twelve equal bars and remove from the pan with a metal spatula.

Nutritional Analysis:
Per brownie: *About 164 calories (6 percent from protein; 52 percent from carbohydrates; 42 percent from fat), 3 grams protein, 23 grams carbohydrates, 8 grams fat (4 grams saturated fat), 28 milligrams cholesterol, 53 milligrams sodium*

Chocolate Chip Cookies

MAKES ABOUT 3 DOZEN

· 💥 ·

New Creaming Method

*I*f you like chocolate chip cookies with crisp edges and chewy centers, these are for you. They're a good illustration of how I devise reduced-fat versions of high-fat classics. Sure, I could have cut out all of the butter, but they wouldn't have resembled chocolate chip cookies.

Nonstick canola oil spray

1 ½ cups unbleached all-purpose flour (*spoon* into measuring cup and level top)
1 teaspoon baking soda
⅛ teaspoon salt

½ cup packed dark brown sugar
½ cup granulated sugar
4 tablespoons (½ stick) unsalted butter, at room temperature

1 large egg
1 tablespoon canola oil
1 tablespoon light corn syrup
2 teaspoons vanilla extract

½ cup mini-chocolate chips

1. Position a rack in the center of the oven and preheat to 350° F. Lightly spray two nonstick baking sheets (preferably insulated) with oil.

2. In a medium bowl, whisk the flour, baking soda, and salt until well combined. Set aside.

3. In a medium bowl, using a handheld electric mixer set at high speed, scraping down the sides of the bowl often with a rubber spatula to force the mixture into the blades, beat the brown sugar, granulated sugar, and butter until the mixture resembles coarse bread crumbs, about 1 ½ minutes.

4. In a small bowl, beat the egg, oil, corn syrup, and vanilla. Pour into the butter/sugar mixture and beat until combined. Add the dry ingredients and the chocolate chips. Using a spoon, stir just until a stiff dough forms.

5. Using a heaping teaspoon for each, roll the dough into 1-inch balls. Place them 2 inches apart on the prepared baking sheets. (The cookies will spread during baking.)

6. One sheet at a time, bake until the cookies are lightly browned, 10 to 12 minutes. The cookies will seem soft, but they will crisp as they cool. Cool in the pan for 1 minute, then transfer the cookies to a wire cake rack to cool completely.

....

Nutritional Analysis:

Per cookie: *About 70 calories (5 percent from protein; 64 percent from carbohydrates; 31 percent from fat), 1 gram protein, 12 grams carbohydrates, 3 grams fat (less than 1 gram saturated fat), 9 milligrams cholesterol, 34 milligrams sodium*

Cocoa Crisps

MAKES ABOUT 4 DOZEN COOKIES

· ❋ ·

New Creaming Method

I can't get enough of icebox-type sugar cookies. Dutch-process cocoa gives them an especially dark color and smooth flavor.

Nonstick canola oil spray

1 ¼ cups unbleached all-purpose flour
   (*spoon* into measuring cup and level top)
¼ cup Dutch-process cocoa powder
1 ½ teaspoons baking powder
⅛ teaspoon salt

1 cup sugar
6 tablespoons (¾ stick) unsalted butter,
   at room temperature
1 large egg
1 tablespoon light corn syrup
1 tablespoon vanilla extract

1. In a medium bowl, whisk the flour, cocoa, baking powder, and salt until well combined. If the cocoa is lumpy, sift it into the bowl. Set aside.

2. In a medium bowl, using a handheld electric mixer set at medium speed, scraping down the sides of the bowl often with a rubber spatula to force the mixture into the blades, beat the sugar and the butter until the mixture resembles coarse bread crumbs, about 1 ½ minutes. Add the egg, corn syrup, and vanilla and beat until smooth. Using a spoon, gradually stir in the flour mixture. Transfer to a sheet of waxed paper and form into a log about 12 inches long and 1 inch in diameter. Wrap the log of dough in waxed paper and refrigerate until well chilled, at least 2 hours or overnight.

3. Position a rack in the center of the oven and preheat to 375° F. Lightly spray two nonstick cookie sheets (preferably insulated) with oil.

4. Unwrap the chilled dough. Using a thin, sharp knife, cut the dough into ¼-inch-thick rounds. Place 2 inches apart on the prepared baking sheets.

5. One sheet at a time, bake the cookies until lightly browned around the edges, 10 to 12 minutes. The centers may seem lightly undone, but they will firm when cooled. Cool on the pans for 1 minute, then transfer to a wire cake rack to cool completely.

Nutritional Analysis:
Per cookie: *About 44 calories (5 percent from protein; 63 percent from carbohydrates; 32 percent from fat), 1 gram protein, 7 grams carbohydrates, 2 grams fat (1 gram saturated fat), 8 milligrams cholesterol, 18 milligrams sodium*

Whole Wheat Fig Bars

MAKES ABOUT 20 BARS

· ❋ ·

*f*ruity, chewy, and generously proportioned, here are fig bars that no one will believe are low-fat. While I am a big fan of the fig filling, especially made with moist, plump Calimyrna figs, sometimes I just mix together whatever dried fruits I have in the cupboard—prunes, apricots, raisins, dates, cranberries, the more the merrier. But keep in mind that dates are quite sweet, and unless you like very sweet foods, don't overdo them. Allow a couple of hours for the crust to chill and the filling to cool.

CRUST
> ³⁄₄ cup unbleached all-purpose flour (*spoon* into measuring cup and level top)
> ³⁄₄ cup whole wheat *pastry* flour (*spoon* into measuring cup and level top)
> ¹⁄₂ cup sugar
> ³⁄₄ teaspoon baking powder
> ¹⁄₈ teaspoon baking soda
> ¹⁄₂ teaspoon ground cinnamon
> Pinch of salt
> 2 tablespoons unsalted butter, chilled
>
> 2 tablespoons low-fat buttermilk
> 1 large egg yolk
> 2 tablespoons ice water, as needed

FILLING
> ¹⁄₂ cup orange juice, apple juice, or water
> 2 tablespoons dark brown sugar
> Grated zest of 1 lemon or ¹⁄₄ teaspoon pure lemon oil
> 1 tablespoon fresh lemon juice

1 tablespoon cornstarch

6 ounces (about 1 cup) coarsely chopped dried
    Calimyrna figs

$\frac{1}{2}$ teaspoon vanilla extract

1. Using the large holes of a box grater, shred the chilled butter onto a plate and freeze for 10 minutes.

2. To make the crust, in a medium bowl, whisk the flours, sugar, baking powder, baking soda, cinnamon, and salt until well combined. Using a pastry blender, cut in the butter until the mixture resembles coarse crumbs.

3. In a small bowl, whisk the buttermilk and egg yolk until combined. Make a well in the center of the dry ingredients and pour in the egg mixture. Stir with a wooden spoon, adding water as needed, to make a soft dough. Place the dough on a piece of waxed paper, pat it into a thick rectangle, and wrap it in the paper. Refrigerate until chilled, about 1 hour.

4. Meanwhile, make the filling. In a medium, heavy-bottomed saucepan, combine the orange juice, brown sugar, lemon zest, and lemon juice. Add the cornstarch and whisk until dissolved. Stir in the chopped figs. Bring to a boil over medium heat, stirring constantly. Cook until the mixture is very thick, about 1 minute. Stir in the vanilla. Transfer to a bowl and let cool completely.

5. Position a rack in the center of the oven and preheat to 350° F. Unwrap the dough and place it between two sheets of waxed paper. Roll it out into a 15 × 7-inch rectangle, about $\frac{1}{4}$ inch thick. Remove the top sheet of waxed paper. Spoon half the cooled filling down the center of the dough, leaving a 1-inch-wide border along the long sides. Bring up the dough to meet over the filling, and pinch the seam and ends closed. Transfer the log of dough, still on the waxed paper, to a nonstick (preferably rimless and insulated) baking sheet. (If the dough seems soft and warm, place pan in freezer for 15 minutes, or until well chilled. Place pan directly from the freezer into a hot oven).

7. Bake until the dough is lightly browned and feels firm when pressed, about 35 minutes. Transfer the pan to a wire cake rack and cool for 20 minutes. Place on a work surface. Using a serrated knife, trim the ends, then slice into bars about ¾ inch thick. Let the bars cool completely on wire cake racks.

Nutritional Analysis:

Per bar: *About 103 calories (7 percent from protein; 79 percent from carbohydrates; 14 percent from fat), 2 grams protein, 21 grams carbohydrates, 2 grams fat (1 gram saturated fat), 14 milligrams cholesterol, 32 milligrams sodium*

Ginger Crackles

· ❋ ·

New Creaming Method

These could be the ultimate ginger cookies—molasses-flavored, crisp, spicy, with a crinkled sugar top. I'm a spice fan, and sometimes I'll add 1 tablespoon minced crystallized ginger or ⅛ teaspoon freshly ground white pepper to the dough for even more spicy punch.

1 ½ cups unbleached all-purpose flour (*spoon* into a
    measuring cup and level top)
1 teaspoon baking soda
1 ½ teaspoons ground cinnamon
1 ½ teaspoons ground ginger
¼ teaspoon ground cloves
⅛ teaspoon salt

1 cup packed dark brown sugar
6 tablespoons (¾ stick) unsalted butter, at room
    temperature
¼ cup unsulphured molasses
1 large egg

2 tablespoons granulated sugar for rolling

1. Position a rack in the center of the oven and preheat to 375° F. Lightly spray two nonstick baking sheets (preferably insulated) with oil.

2. In a small bowl, whisk the flour, baking soda, cinnamon, ginger, cloves, and salt to combine. Set aside.

3. In a medium bowl, using a handheld electric mixer set at medium speed, scraping down the sides of the bowl often with a rubber spatula to force the mixture into the blades, beat the brown sugar and butter until they resemble coarse bread crumbs, about 2 minutes.

Beat in the molasses and the egg. Using a spoon, gradually stir in the flour mixture.

4. Place the granulated sugar in a small bowl. Using a heaping teaspoon for each cookie, roll the dough into 1-inch balls. Roll each ball in the sugar, and place 2 inches apart on a prepared baking sheet. Using the bottom of a flat glass, press the balls gently to flatten them.

5. Bake, one sheet at time, until the tops are crinkled and the edges are set, about 10 minutes. Cool the cookies for 1 minute in the pan, then transfer them to a wire cake rack to cool completely.

Nutritional Analysis:

Per cookie: *About 78 calories (4 percent from protein; 69 percent from carbohydrates; 27 percent from fat), 1 gram protein, 14 grams carbohydrates, 2 grams fat (1 gram saturated fat), 13 milligrams cholesterol, 39 milligrams sodium*

Lemon Cheesecake Bars

MAKES 12 BARS

· ✤ ·

These tangy bars can be eaten out of hand for a cool, refreshing family snack, or served on a dessert plate drizzled with strawberry sauce and garnished with a few fresh berries. Either way, they are a hit with kids or grown-ups.

Nonstick canola oil spray

GRAHAM CRACKER CRUST (page 126)

CHEESECAKE FILLING
  $^1\!/\!_2$ cup sugar
  $^1\!/\!_3$ cup whole wheat *pastry* flour (*spoon* into
    measuring cup and level top)
  2 tablespoons cornstarch

  1 $^1\!/\!_2$ cups nonfat yogurt cheese, made in advance
    (page 251)
  Grated zest of 1 lemon or $^1\!/\!_4$ teaspoon lemon oil
  $^1\!/\!_3$ cup fresh lemon juice
  3 large egg whites

1. Position a rack in the center of the oven and preheat to 350° F. Generously spray an 11 × 7-inch ovenproof glass pan with oil. Press the crust mixture firmly and evenly into the bottom of the prepared pan. Bake the crust until set, 8 to 10 minutes. Remove from the oven. Reduce oven temperature to 300° F.

2. To make the filling, in a small bowl, mix the sugar, flour, and cornstarch. Set aside. Using a handheld electric mixer set at medium speed, beat the yogurt cheese, lemon zest and juice, and the egg whites until smooth, about 1 minute. Using a spoon, stir in the flour mixture. Pour over the prepared crust and smooth the top.

3. Bake until tiny cracks appear in the top of the cheesecake, and the edges are slightly puffed and lightly browned, about 30 to 35 minutes. Do not overbake—the center will seem unset but will firm when cooled. Cool to room temperature in the pan on a wire cake rack. Cover with plastic wrap and refrigerate until chilled, at least 4 hours or overnight.

4. Run a sharp knife inside the pan to release from the sides. Using a sharp knife, cut into twelve bars. Serve chilled. Store, well wrapped, in refrigerator.

Nutritional Analysis:

Per bar: *About 180 calories (10 percent from protein; 69 percent from carbohydrates; 21 percent from fat), 5 grams protein, 31 grams carbohydrates, 4 grams fat (2 grams saturated fat), 8 milligrams cholesterol, 121 milligrams sodium*

Lemon Crisps

· 🌟 ·

New Creaming Method

Similar to the Icebox Sugar Cookies on page 212, these are just different enough to merit their own recipe. Consider substituting grated orange or lime zest or $1/4$ teaspoon pure orange or lime oil and juice for the lemon. If you have pure lemon oil, add it to the dough for a stronger flavor.

Nonstick canola oil spray

1 $1/2$ cups unbleached all-purpose flour (*spoon* into
    measuring cup and level top)
$1/2$ teaspoon baking soda
$1/8$ teaspoon salt

1 cup sugar
6 tablespoons ($3/4$ cup) unsalted butter, at room
    temperature
1 large egg
Grated zest of 1 lemon
1 tablespoon fresh lemon juice
$1/4$ teaspoon pure lemon oil (optional)

2 tablespoons sugar, for dipping

1. In a medium bowl, whisk the flour, baking soda, and salt until well combined. Set aside.

2. In another medium bowl, using a handheld electric mixer set at medium speed, scraping down the sides of the bowl often with a rubber spatula to force the mixture into the blades, beat the sugar and the butter until the mixture resembles coarse bread crumbs, about 1 $1/2$ minutes.

Add the egg, lemon zest and juice, and the lemon oil if using it, and beat until smooth. Using a spoon, gradually stir in the flour mixture. Transfer to a sheet of waxed paper and form into a log about 12 inches long and 1 inch in diameter. Wrap the log of dough in the waxed paper and refrigerate until well chilled, at least 2 hours or overnight.

3. Position a rack in the center of the oven and preheat to 375° F. Lightly spray 2 nonstick cookie sheets (preferably insulated) with oil.

4. Unwrap the chilled dough. Using a thin, sharp knife, cut the dough crosswise into ¼-inch-thick rounds. Place the rounds 2 inches apart on the prepared baking sheets.

5. One sheet at a time, bake the cookies until lightly browned around the edges, 10 to 12 minutes. The centers may seem lightly underdone, but they will firm when cooled. Cool in the pan on a wire cake rack for 1 minute, then transfer to the rack to cool completely.

Nutritional Analysis:

Per cookie: *About 44 calories (5 percent from protein; 63 percent from carbohydrates; 32 percent from fat), 1 gram protein, 7 grams carbohydrates, 2 grams fat (1 gram saturated fat), 8 milligrams cholesterol, 16 milligrams sodium*

Florida Lime Bars

MAKES 12 BARS

· ❋ ·

*I*n Florida, Key lime pies are always made with local Key lime juice. There weren't many cows in the Keys in the early days, so most Key lime pies are made with condensed milk. Until the advent of low-fat condensed milk, I rarely made these pies, but now I've turned them into one of my favorite bar cookies. Because Key limes are rare outside Florida, and I don't care for the bottled juice, I make these with fresh limes of the Tahiti or Persian varieties.

Nonstick canola oil spray

GRAHAM CRACKER CRUST (page 126)

FILLING
    3 tablespoons sugar
    2 tablespoons cornstarch
    One 14–ounce can low-fat sweetened condensed milk
    1 large egg
    Grated zest of 1 lime
    1/2 cup fresh lime juice
    1/4 teaspoon pure lime oil (optional)

1. Position a rack in the center of the oven and preheat to 325° F. Lightly spray an 8-inch square nonstick baking pan with vegetable oil spray.

2. Press the crust mixture firmly and evenly into the bottom of the prepared pan.

3. To make the filling, in a medium bowl, combine the sugar and cornstarch. Gradually stir in the condensed milk, and then the egg. Add the lime zest, juice, and lime oil, if using it, and stir just until combined. Pour over the crust.

4. Bake until the edges look firm, but the center is still slightly unset, about 25 minutes. Cool in the pan on a wire cake rack to room temperature. Cover with plastic wrap and refrigerate until chilled, at least 2 hours or overnight.

5. To serve, run a knife inside the pan to release from the sides. Using a knife, cut into twelve equal bars. Serve chilled. To store, wrap well and keep refrigerated.

Nutritional Analysis:
Per bar: *About 231 calories (7 percent from protein; 70 percent from carbohydrates; 22 percent from fat), 4 grams protein, 40 grams carbohydrates, 6 grams fat (2 grams saturated fat), 30 milligrams cholesterol, 117 milligrams sodium*

Oatmeal Cowboy Cookies

MAKES ABOUT 3 DOZEN COOKIES

New Creaming Method

My siblings, Stephen, Sue, and Diana, make chunky oatmeal cookies that are loaded with chocolate chips, nuts, eggs, and butter. When we wanted to make them over, it was a matter of reducing the fat until I still got a great cookie. They aren't quite "diet food," but they have a much slimmer profile than the original.

Nonstick canola oil spray

1 cup unbleached all-purpose flour (*spoon* into measuring cup and level top)
¾ cup quick-cooking oatmeal
1 teaspoon baking powder
½ teaspoon baking soda
⅛ teaspoon salt

1 cup packed dark brown sugar
6 tablespoons (¾ stick) unsalted butter, at room temperature
1 large egg
1 tablespoon vanilla extract

½ cup raisins
¼ cup chocolate chips, coarsely chopped
¼ cup chopped walnuts

1. Position a rack in the center of the oven and preheat to 375° F. Lightly spray two nonstick baking sheets (preferably insulated) with oil.

2. In a medium bowl, whisk the flour, oatmeal, baking powder, baking soda, and salt until well combined. Set aside.

3. In another medium bowl, using a handheld electric mixer set at high speed, scraping down the sides of the bowl often with a rubber spatula to force the mixture into the blades, beat the brown sugar and butter until the mixture resembles coarse crumbs, about 1 ½ minutes. Add the egg and vanilla and beat until smooth. Using a spoon, gradually stir in the dry ingredients, adding the raisins, chocolate chips, and walnuts with the last addition.

4. Drop heaping teaspoonfuls of dough, 2 inches apart, on the prepared baking sheets.

5. One sheet at a time, bake until the cookies are lightly browned around the edges, 10 to 12 minutes. The cookies will seem soft, but they will crisp as they cool. Cool in the pans for 1 minute, then transfer to a wire cake rack to cool completely.

Nutritional Analysis:
Per cookie: *About 78 calories (6 percent calories from protein; 61 percent from carbohydrates; 33 percent from fat), 1 gram protein, 12 grams carbohydrates, 3 grams fat (1 gram saturated fat), 11 milligrams cholesterol, 33 milligrams sodium*

Oatmeal Raisin Cookies

MAKES ABOUT 4 DOZEN COOKIES

· 🟊 ·

New Creaming Method

*M*y stepmother, Beverly, makes these cookies for my dad, Henry. They're everything an oatmeal cookie should be—crunchy and chewy at the same time.

Nonstick canola oil spray

1 cup unbleached all-purpose flour (*spoon* into measuring cup and level top)

²⁄₃ cup quick-cooking oatmeal

2 tablespoons cornstarch

1 teaspoon baking soda

1 teaspoon ground cinnamon

¹⁄₈ teaspoon salt

¹⁄₂ cup packed dark brown sugar

¹⁄₂ cup granulated sugar

2 tablespoons unsalted butter, at room temperature

3 large egg whites

1 tablespoon light corn syrup

1 tablespoon canola oil

1 tablespoon vanilla extract

¹⁄₂ cup raisins

1. Position a rack in the center of the oven and preheat to 350° F. Lightly spray two nonstick baking sheets (preferably insulated) with oil.

2. In a medium bowl, whisk the flour, oatmeal, cornstarch, baking soda, cinnamon, and salt until well combined. Set aside.

3. In another medium bowl, using a handheld electric mixer set at

high speed, scraping down the sides of the bowl often with a rubber spatula to force the mixture into the blades, beat the brown sugar, granulated sugar, and butter until the mixture resembles coarse bread crumbs, about 1 $\frac{1}{2}$ minutes.

4. In a small bowl, beat the egg whites, corn syrup, oil, and vanilla. Pour into the butter/sugar mixture and beat until combined. Add the dry ingredients and the raisins. Using a spoon, stir just until a stiff dough forms.

5. Drop heaping teaspoonfuls of dough about 2 inches apart onto the prepared baking sheets. (The cookies will spread out during baking.)

6. One sheet at a time, bake until the edges are lightly browned, 8 to 10 minutes. The cookies will seem soft, but they will crisp as they cool. Cool in the pan for 5 minutes, then transfer to a wire cake rack to cool completely.

Nutritional Analysis:
Per cookie: *About 46 calories (6 percent calories from protein; 77 percent from carbohydrates; 17 percent from fat), 1 gram protein, 9 grams carbohydrates, 1 gram fat (less than 1 gram saturated fat), 1 milligram cholesterol, 27 milligrams sodium*

Zesty Orange-Coconut Bars

MAKES 18 BARS

· ✳ ·

New Classic Method

Cookie lovers with more sophisticated taste will appreciate these elegant bars. On the other hand, they seem to disappear when kids are around, too.

Nonstick canola oil spray

1 ½ cups unbleached all-purpose flour (*spoon* into
   measuring cup and level top)
½ cup sweetened coconut flakes
¼ teaspoon baking powder
¼ teaspoon baking soda
⅛ teaspoon salt

½ cup sugar
1 large egg
2 tablespoons buttermilk
2 tablespoons canola oil
1 teaspoon vanilla extract
Grated zest of 1 orange or ¼ teaspoon pure orange oil

¾ cup orange all-fruit spread
2 tablespoons fresh orange juice
2 tablespoons sweetened coconut flakes

1. Position a rack in the center of the oven and preheat to 350° F. Lightly spray an 11 × 7-inch nonstick pan with oil.

2. In a medium bowl, whisk the flour, ½ cup coconut, baking powder, baking soda, and salt until well combined. Set aside.

3. In another medium bowl, whisk together the sugar, egg, buttermilk, oil, vanilla, and orange zest. Make a well in the center of the dry ingredients and pour in the buttermilk mixture. Stir until the dough is completely moistened, but crumbly. Press firmly and evenly into the prepared pan.

4. Bake until the dough is golden brown and the top feels dry, 20 to 25 minutes. Remove from the oven. In a small bowl, whisk the orange spread and orange juice. Spread over the crust and sprinkle with the 2 tablespoons coconut. Return to the oven and bake until the orange spread bubbles around the edges, 10 to 15 minutes. Cool completely in the pan on a wire cake rack.

5. Run a knife inside the pan. Using a knife, cut into eighteen bars. Serve chilled.

....

Nutritional Analysis:
Per bar: *About 114 calories (5 percent from protein; 74 percent from carbohydrates; 20 percent from fat), 2 grams protein, 21 grams carbohydrates, 3 grams fat (less than 1 gram saturated fat), 12 milligrams cholesterol, 37 milligrams sodium*

Peanut Butter Crisscross Cookies

MAKES ABOUT 2 1/2 DOZEN COOKIES

· ✳ ·

New Creaming Method

These rich-tasting crunchy peanut butter cookies from our family recipe box have been judiciously trimmed. I cut only 6 tablespoons of butter and 1/4 cup of peanut butter, which amounted to 100 grams of fat and 976 calories per batch! Actually, reducing the amount of butter resulted in a more peanuty cookie!

Nonstick canola oil spray

1 cup unbleached all-purpose flour (*spoon* into
   measuring cup and level top)
1/2 teaspoon baking soda
1/8 teaspoon salt

3/4 cup chunky peanut butter, preferably natural-style
1/3 cup granulated sugar
1/3 cup packed dark brown sugar
2 tablespoons unsalted butter, at room temperature
1 large egg
1 tablespoon corn syrup
1 tablespoon vanilla extract

1. Position a rack in the center of the oven and preheat to 350° F. Lightly spray two nonstick baking sheets (preferably insulated) with oil.

2. In a small bowl, whisk the flour, baking soda, and salt until well combined. Set aside.

3. In a medium bowl, using a handheld electric mixer set at medium speed, beat the peanut butter, granulated sugar, brown sugar, and butter until well mixed, about 2 minutes. Beat in the egg, corn syrup, and vanilla. Stir in the flour mixture.

4. Using about 1 teaspoon for each, roll the dough into balls. Place the balls about 2 inches apart on the prepared baking sheets. Using a fork, press the dough with a crisscross pattern, to flatten the balls.

5. Bake 1 sheet at a time, until the edges are lightly browned, 8 to 10 minutes. The centers may seem slightly underdone but they will firm when cooled. Cool in the pan for 1 minute, then transfer to a wire cake rack to cool completely.

Nutritional Analysis:
Per cookie: *About 78 calories (10 percent from protein; 47 percent from carbohydrates; 43 percent from fat), 2 grams protein, 9 grams carbohydrates, 4 grams fat (less than 1 gram saturated fat), 9 milligrams cholesterol, 27 milligrams sodium*

Pumpkin Cheesecake Bars

MAKES 12 BARS

· ✳ ·

Nonfat yogurt cheese and pumpkin give these bars their thick, creamy body. They are a wonderful autumn treat. Allow time for chilling overnight.

Nonstick canola oil spray

GRAHAM CRACKER CRUST (page 126)

$1/3$ **cup whole wheat** *pastry* **flour (***spoon* **into measuring cup and level top)**

2 tablespoons cornstarch

1 teaspoon ground cinnamon

$1/2$ **teaspoon ground nutmeg**

$1/4$ **teaspoon ground ginger**

$1/8$ **teaspoon salt**

1 cup nonfat yogurt cheese, made in advance (page 251)

$3/4$ **cup canned pumpkin**

$1/2$ **cup sugar**

3 large egg whites

1. Position a rack in the center of the oven and preheat to 350° F. Generously spray an 11 × 7-inch ovenproof glass baking pan with oil. Press the crust mixture firmly and evenly into the bottom of the prepared pan. Bake until the crust looks set, 8 to 10 minutes. Remove the pan from the oven. Reduce the oven temperature to 300° F.

2. In a small bowl, mix the flour, cornstarch, cinnamon, nutmeg, ginger, and salt until well combined. Set aside.

3. In a medium bowl, using a handheld electric mixer set at medium speed, beat the yogurt cheese, pumpkin, sugar, and egg whites just until combined, about 1 minute. Using a spoon, stir in the flour mixture. Pour the batter into the prepared crust and smooth the top.

4. Bake just until a few tiny cracks appear on the surface and the edges are puffed and lightly browned, about 40 to 45 minutes. Do not overbake—the center will seem unset, but will firm when chilled. Cool to room temperature in the pan on a wire cake rack. Cover with plastic wrap and refrigerate until chilled, at least 4 hours or overnight.

5. Run a sharp knife inside the pan to release the cheesecake bars from the sides. Using a sharp knife, cut into twelve bars. Serve chilled. Store, well wrapped, in refrigerator.

Nutritional Analysis:

Per bar: *About 184 calories (10 percent from protein; 69 percent from carbohydrates; 21 percent from fat), 5 grams protein, 32 grams carbohydrates, 4 grams fat (2 grams saturated fat), 8 milligrams cholesterol, 144 milligrams sodium*

Icebox Sugar Cookies

MAKES ABOUT 4 DOZEN COOKIES

· ✳ ·

New Creaming Method

These chill-and-bake cookies have a high nostalgia factor—they are the kinds of simple, crispy vanilla cookies I must have eaten by the dozens when I was growing up. The basic recipe, reduced in fat and calories, will disappear from your cookie jar, but my family also likes the spiced version. My son Alex loves to make them with me, but he loves to eat them even more. Allow at least 2 hours to chill the dough.

Nonstick canola oil spray

1 ½ cups unbleached all-purpose flour
   (*spoon* into measuring cup and level top)
1 ½ teaspoons baking powder
⅛ teaspoon salt

1 cup sugar
6 tablespoons (¾ stick) unsalted butter, at
   room temperature
1 large egg
1 tablespoon light corn syrup
1 tablespoon vanilla extract

2 tablespoons sugar for dipping

1. In a medium bowl, whisk the flour, baking powder, and salt until well combined. Set aside.

2. In another medium bowl, using a handheld electric mixer set at medium speed, scraping down the sides of the bowl often with a rubber spatula to force the mixture into the blades, beat the 1 cup of sugar and the butter until the mixture resembles coarse bread crumbs, about 1 ½ minutes. Add the egg, corn syrup, and vanilla and beat until smooth. Using a spoon, gradually stir in the flour mixture. Transfer the dough to a sheet of waxed paper and form it into a log about 12 inches long and 1 inch in diameter. Wrap the log of dough in the waxed paper and refrigerate until well chilled, at least 2 hours or overnight.

3. Position a rack in the center of the oven and preheat to 375° F. Lightly spray 2 nonstick cookie sheets (preferably insulated) with oil.

4. Unwrap the chilled dough. Place the 2 tablespoons of sugar in a small bowl. Using a thin, sharp knife, cut the dough crosswise into ¼-inch-thick rounds. Dip each round in the sugar, and place the cookies, sugar side up, 2 inches apart on the prepared baking sheets.

5. One sheet at a time, bake the cookies until lightly browned around the edges, 10 to 12 minutes. The centers may seem slightly underdone, but they will firm when cooled. Cool the cookies in the pan for 1 minute, then transfer to a wire cake rack to cool completely.

SPICY CINNAMON COOKIES: Add 1 teaspoon ground cinnamon to the dry ingredients. Stir ¼ teaspoon ground cinnamon and ⅛ teaspoon ground cloves into the 2 tablespoons of sugar for dipping.

Nutritional Analysis:
Per cookie (including Spicy Cinnamon Cookies): *About 48 calories (5 percent from protein; 66 percent from carbohydrates; 29 percent from fat), 1 gram protein, 8 grams carbohydrates, 2 grams fat (1 gram saturated fat), 8 milligrams cholesterol, 12 milligrams sodium*

The Fruit Basket:
Cobblers, Buckles,
and Friends

Baked Apples
with Cranberry Filling

MAKES 6 SERVINGS

· ❋ ·

When winter winds blow, baked apples are a comforting dessert. Enjoy them plain, with just their cooking liquid spooned on top, or add a scoop of vanilla frozen yogurt. Rome apples keep their shape during baking, and are the best choice.

> **6 Rome apples (about 9 ounces each)**
> **1 lemon, cut in half**
> **¹/₂ cup fresh bread crumbs**
> **¹/₂ cup dried cranberries**
> **1 tablespoon sugar**
> **1 tablespoon unsalted butter, chilled, cut into**
>   **small pieces**
> **¹/₄ teaspoon ground allspice**
> **¹/₄ teaspoon ground cinnamon**
> **2 cups unsweetened apple juice**
> **¹/₃ cup pure maple syrup, preferably grade B**
> **1 tablespoon cornstarch**
> **1 tablespoon water**

1. Position a rack in the center of the oven and preheat to 350° F. Generously spray a 9 × 13-inch ovenproof glass baking dish with oil.

2. Using a vegetable peeler, remove the top 1¹/₂ inches of peel from each apple, rubbing the peeled apple with the halved lemon. Using the tip of the peeler, dig out the core, reaching almost, but not quite all the way, to the bottom of the apple. Arrange the apples in the baking dish. Squeeze the remaining lemon juice all over the apples, especially into the cored areas.

3. In a small bowl, mix the bread crumbs, cranberries, sugar, butter, allspice, and cinnamon. Stuff the apples with the crumb mixture. Pour the apple juice into the baking dish. Drizzle the maple syrup all over the apples.

4. Bake, basting occasionally, until the apples are tender when pierced with the tip of a knife, about 50 minutes. Using a slotted spoon, transfer the apples to individual soup dishes.

5. In a small saucepan, sprinkle the cornstarch over the 1 tablespoon of water and stir to dissolve. Whisk in the juices from the baking dish. Bring to a boil over medium heat, stirring occasionally, just until lightly thickened. Pour equal amounts of syrup over the apples. Serve immediately.

Nutritional Analysis:
Per serving: *About 310 calories (1 percent from protein; 90 percent from carbohydrates; 9 percent from fat), 1 gram protein, 75 grams carbohydrates, 3 grams fat (1 gram saturated fat), 5 milligrams cholesterol, 42 milligrams sodium*

Apple-Berry Crisp with Maple Crunch

MAKES 9 SERVINGS

· ✴ ·

$\mathcal{A}$t first glance, this looks like an easy dessert to whip up for a family supper. And it is! But my son Tom loves the leftovers for breakfast, and sometimes on a weekend, I'll serve it to everyone instead of plain old granola and fruit. For dessert, serve it with frozen yogurt, but for breakfast, regular yogurt is perfect. The crunchy oatmeal topping is absolutely irresistible.

Nonstick canola oil spray

6 medium Golden Delicious apples, peeled, cored, and cut into $\frac{1}{2}$-inch wedges

1 cup fresh or frozen (do not thaw) blueberries or raspberries

1 cup unsweetened applesauce

1 $\frac{1}{2}$ cups quick-cooking oatmeal

$\frac{1}{3}$ cup plus 1 tablespoon pure maple syrup, preferably grade B

$\frac{1}{3}$ cup plus 1 tablespoon unbleached all-purpose flour (*spoon* into measuring cup and level top, then measure 1 level tablespoon)

3 tablespoons fresh lemon juice

1 $\frac{1}{2}$ tablespoons canola oil

1 $\frac{1}{2}$ teaspoons vanilla extract

1 teaspoon ground cinnamon

$\frac{1}{8}$ teaspoon ground nutmeg

1 tablespoon sugar

1. Position a rack in the center of the oven and preheat to 350° F. Generously spray a 9 × 13-inch ovenproof glass baking pan with oil.

2. Place the apples and blueberries in the prepared pan and spread with the applesauce. In a medium bowl, stir the oatmeal, syrup, flour, lemon juice, oil, vanilla, cinnamon, and nutmeg until well combined. Crumble the mixture over the fruit and sprinkle with the sugar.

3. Bake until the apples are tender and the topping is browned, about 45 minutes. Serve hot or warm.

Nutritional Analysis:
Per serving: *About 206 calories (6 percent from protein; 80 percent from carbohydrates; 15 percent from fat), 3 grams protein, 43 grams carbohydrates, 4 grams fat (less than 1 gram saturated fat), 0 milligrams cholesterol, 16 milligrams sodium*

Blackberry Cobbler

MAKES 8 SERVINGS

· ✳ ·

New Class ic Method

*T*his is a traditional cobbler with drop biscuits for topping. Vary the berries to use your favorite—a combination of raspberries, blueberries, and blackberries is especially good. Each serving has almost 4 grams of fiber.

BERRIES

4 cups fresh or frozen (do not thaw) blackberries

¼ cup sugar

2 tablespoons cornstarch

1 tablespoon fresh lemon juice (optional)

COBBLER DOUGH

1 cup whole wheat *pastry* flour (*spoon* into measuring cup and level top)

¾ teaspoon baking powder

½ teaspoon baking soda

⅛ teaspoon salt

⅓ cup low-fat buttermilk

2 tablespoons sugar

1 large egg

1 ½ teaspoons canola oil

½ teaspoon vanilla extract

1. Position a rack in the center of the oven and preheat to 350° F. Generously spray an 11 × 7-inch ovenproof glass baking pan with oil.

2. In a medium bowl, toss together the blackberries, sugar, cornstarch, and lemon juice, if using. Transfer to the prepared baking dish. Set aside.

3. In another medium bowl, whisk the flour, baking powder, baking soda, and salt until well combined. Set aside.

4. In a third medium bowl, using a handheld electric mixer set at high speed, beat the buttermilk, sugar, egg, oil, and vanilla until frothy, about 2 minutes. Make a well in the center of the dry ingredients and pour in the buttermilk mixture. Stir with a wooden spoon just until combined. Do not overmix.

5. Drop large tablespoonfuls of the batter over the berries. Bake until the topping is golden brown, about 30 minutes. Do not overbake. Cool slightly in the pan on a wire cake rack, then serve warm.

Nutritional Analysis:

Per serving: *About 238 calories (10 percent from protein; 77 percent from carbohydrates; 12 percent from fat), 6 grams protein, 48 grams carbohydrates, 3 grams fat (less than 1 gram saturated fat), 28 milligrams cholesterol, 238 milligrams sodium*

Blueberry Buckle

· ✻ ·

New Creaming Method

*M*outhwatering is the only word to describe plump berries in a tender cake, topped with a crumb streusel. You can use other berries, of course, such as raspberries or blackberries, but blueberry buckle is a classic. I often double the topping recipe.

Nonstick canola oil spray

TOPPING

$^1/_4$ cup sugar

1 tablespoon cake flour, *not* self-rising

1 tablespoon unsalted butter, at room temperature

$^1/_4$ teaspoon ground cinnamon

Large pinch of ground nutmeg (optional)

BUCKLE

2 tablespoons unsalted butter, at room temperature

$^1/_2$ cup sugar

$^1/_4$ cup 1 percent low-fat milk

1 large egg

1 tablespoon nonfat dry milk powder (do not reconstitute)

$^1/_2$ teaspoon vanilla extract

$^1/_8$ teaspoon almond extract (optional)

1 cup unbleached cake flour, *not* self-rising (*spoon* into measuring cup and level top)

1 teaspoon baking powder

Pinch of salt

$^1/_2$ cup fresh or frozen (do not thaw) blueberries

1. Position a rack in the center of the oven and preheat to 350° F. Lightly spray an 8-inch nonstick round cake pan with oil.

2. To make the topping, in a small bowl, rub the sugar, flour, butter, cinnamon, and nutmeg, if using it, with your fingers until combined and crumbly. Set aside.

3. In a medium bowl, using a handheld electric mixer set at medium-high speed, scraping down the sides of the bowl often with a rubber spatula to force the mixture into the blades, beat the butter and sugar until the mixture resembles coarse bread crumbs, about 1 ½ minutes.

4. In another medium bowl, beat the milk, egg, nonfat dry milk powder, vanilla, and almond extract, if using it, until combined. Pour into the butter-sugar mixture and beat just until combined.

5. In a third medium bowl, whisk the flour, baking powder, and salt to combine. In three additions, stir the flour mixture into the wet ingredients. Fold in the blueberries. Pour into the prepared pan. Gently smooth the top and sprinkle with the reserved topping.

6. Bake until the top of the buckle springs back when pressed in the center and the sides are lightly browned and pulling away from the pan, 25 to 30 minutes. Cool in the pan on a wire cake rack. Serve warm or at room temperature.

....

Nutritional Analysis:
Per serving: *About 181 calories (5 percent from protein; 70 percent from carbohydrates; 25 percent from fat), 2 grams protein, 33 grams carbohydrates, 5 grams fat (3 grams saturated fat), 39 milligrams cholesterol, 84 milligrams sodium*

Blueberry Soufflé

MAKES 4 SERVINGS

· ✻ ·

$\mathcal{A}$ soufflé is grown-up food. This hot blueberry version is a lovely dessert to serve at a special dinner party with close friends. It is really quite easy to make, and will become a staple in your repertoire. You can substitute raspberries or blackberries, if you wish.

Nonstick canola oil spray

$^{1}/_{2}$ cup plus 2 tablespoons sugar
3 cups fresh or frozen (do not thaw)
   blueberries
1 tablespoon fresh lemon juice
5 large egg whites, at room temperature
   (see page 253)

1. Position a rack in the center of the oven and preheat to 375° F. Generously spray a 2-quart soufflé mold with oil. Sprinkle 2 tablespoons of the sugar into the mold, and turn it to coat with the sugar. Tap out the excess sugar.

2. In a blender, puree the blueberries, remaining $^{1}/_{2}$ cup sugar, and lemon juice. In a medium saucepan over medium heat, bring to a simmer, stirring often. Set aside $^{3}/_{4}$ cup of the puree.

3. In a large, grease-free bowl, using a handheld electric mixer set at low speed, beat the egg whites until foamy. Increase the speed to high and beat until soft peaks form. Stir about one fourth of the beaten whites into the puree in the saucepan. Fold in the remaining whites with a large rubber spatula. Gently pour the mixture into the prepared mold.

4. Bake until the top of the soufflé is golden brown and a long skewer inserted in the center comes out clean, 20 to 25 minutes. Meanwhile, reheat the reserved puree.

5. Present the soufflé at the table and serve immediately, spooning some of the warm sauce over each portion.

Nutritional Analysis:
Per serving: *About 196 calories (10 percent from protein; 88 percent from carbohydrates; 2 percent from fat), 5 grams protein, 46 grams carbohydrates, less than 1 gram fat (0 grams saturated fat), 0 milligrams cholesterol, 76 milligrams sodium*

Two-Berry Crumble

MAKES 10 SERVINGS

· ❋ ·

When both raspberries and blueberries are in season, I like to mix them for a summery treat.

Nonstick canola oil spray

FILLING

1 cup fresh or frozen (do not thaw) blueberries
1 cup fresh or frozen (do not thaw) raspberries
¼ cup granulated sugar
Grated zest of 1 lemon or ¼ teaspoon lemon oil
2 tablespoons fresh lemon juice

CRUMBLE TOPPING

1 cup unbleached all-purpose flour (*spoon* into measuring cup and level top)
1 cup packed dark brown sugar
1 teaspoon ground cinnamon
1 teaspoon freshly grated nutmeg
2 tablespoons unsalted butter, at room temperature

1. Position a rack in the center of the oven and preheat the oven to 375° F. Generously spray a 9-inch ovenproof glass pie pan with oil.

2. To make the filling, in the prepared pan, toss the berries, granulated sugar, lemon zest, and lemon juice. Set aside.

3. To make the crumble topping, in a medium bowl, mix the flour, brown sugar, cinnamon, and nutmeg. Using a pastry blender or your fingertips, blend the butter into the dry ingredients until the mixture resembles coarse bread crumbs. Sprinkle over the berries.

4. Bake until the blueberries are bubbling, 20 to 25 minutes. Serve warm.

MANGO-RASPBERRY CRUMBLE: Substitute 1 fresh ripe mango, peeled, pitted, and cut into ¹/₂-inch chunks, for the blueberries. Substitute lime zest and juice for the lemon.

Nutritional Analyses

Two-Berry Crumble (per serving): *About 182 calories (3 percent from protein; 84 percent from carbohydrates; 13 percent from fat), 2 grams protein, 39 grams carbohydrates, 3 grams fat (2 grams saturated fat), 6 milligrams cholesterol, 7 milligrams sodium*

Mango-Raspberry Crumble (per serving): *About 188 calories (3 percent from protein; 85 percent from carbohydrates; 12 percent from fat), 2 grams protein, 41 grams carbohydrates, 3 grams fat (2 grams saturated fat), 6 milligrams cholesterol, 8 milligrams sodium*

Honey-and-Ginger Pear Betty

MAKES 6 SERVINGS

· ✻ ·

A fruit betty is layered with bread crumbs, which soak up and thicken the juices. Make bread crumbs in a food processor or blender from day-old, firm sandwich bread and don't bother to trim the crusts. Use cinnamon-raisin bread if you have some—it's outrageous! Just crumble the raisin bread as finely as possible in your hands. This is delicious served as is, warm from the oven, or embellish it with frozen vanilla yogurt, Vanilla Custard Sauce (page 141) or New "Whipped Cream" (page 138).

5 large ripe Anjou pears, peeled, cored, and cut into
   $\frac{1}{2}$ inch-thick slices
$\frac{1}{4}$ cup honey
2 tablespoons minced crystallized ginger or 1 teaspoon
   ground ginger
1 tablespoon fresh lemon juice

1 cup fresh bread crumbs, made from about 3 slices
   bread
$\frac{2}{3}$ cup packed dark brown sugar
1 teaspoon ground cinnamon
1 tablespoon unsalted butter, cut into small pieces

1. Position a rack in the center of the oven and preheat to 350° F. Spray an 8-inch square ovenproof glass pan with oil.

2. In a large bowl, toss the pears with the honey, ginger, and lemon juice. Set aside.

3. In a medium bowl, toss the bread crumbs, brown sugar, and cinnamon. Sprinkle one third of the crumbs into the prepared baking dish. Top with half the pear slices. Sprinkle with half the remaining crumbs, then top with the remaining pears. Finish with the remaining crumbs and dot with the butter.

4. Bake until the pears are tender and the topping is lightly browned, 35 to 40 minutes. Serve warm.

Nutritional Analysis:

Per serving: *About 236 calories (2 percent from protein; 88 percent from carbohydrates; 10 percent from fat), 1 gram protein, 55 grams carbohydrates, 3 grams fat (1 gram saturated fat), 3 milligrams cholesterol, 44 milligrams sodium*

Colonial Raspberry-Almond Slump

MAKES 8 SERVINGS

· ✳ ·

New Class Method

What we might call a cobbler, colonial American cooks called a slump (probably because it "slumps" in a bowl instead of standing straight up on a plate). Slump is a not-so-attractive name for a wonderful dessert. Serve it warm with a scoop of frozen vanilla yogurt or a spoonful of Vanilla Custard Sauce (page 141).

Nonstick canola oil spray

FILLING
3 tablespoons water
Grated zest of 1 lemon or $^1\!/_4$ teaspoon pure lemon oil
1 tablespoon fresh lemon juice
3 tablespoons sugar
1 $^1\!/_2$ teaspoons cornstarch
3 cups fresh or frozen (do not thaw) raspberries

TOPPING
1 $^1\!/_4$ cups whole wheat *pastry* flour (*spoon* into
    measuring cup and level top)
$^3\!/_4$ teaspoon baking powder
$^1\!/_2$ teaspoon ground cinnamon
Pinch of salt

$^1\!/_2$ cup packed dark brown sugar
$^1\!/_3$ cup plus 1 tablespoon low-fat buttermilk
$^1\!/_3$ cup plus 1 tablespoon unsweetened applesauce
1 large egg

1 teaspoon vanilla extract
¼ teaspoon almond extract

2 tablespoons sliced almonds for topping

1. Position a rack in the center of the oven and preheat to 350° F. Generously spray a 10-inch deep-dish ovenproof glass pie pan or a 9-inch round nonstick baking pan with oil. (You can use a 9-inch pie pan, but place it on a baking sheet to catch any raspberry juices that may bubble over during baking.)

2. To make the filling, in a medium bowl, stir the water with the lemon zest and juice. Add the sugar and cornstarch and stir to dissolve the cornstarch. Add the berries and toss. Pour into the prepared pie pan.

3. In another medium bowl, whisk the flour, baking powder, cinnamon, and salt to combine well. Set aside.

4. In a third medium bowl, using a handheld electric mixer set at high speed, beat the brown sugar, buttermilk, applesauce, egg, vanilla, and almond extract until light in color and foamy, about 2 minutes. Make a well in the center of the dry ingredients. Pour the buttermilk mixture into the well. Stir with a spoon just until combined. Do not overmix. Drop large spoonfuls of the batter around the edges of the pan, and lightly spoon small dollops over the fruit in the center. Sprinkle with the almonds.

5. Bake until the fruit is bubbling and the top of the cake springs back when pressed lightly, 25 to 30 minutes. Do not overbake. Serve warm.

Nutritional Analysis:
Per serving: *About 195 calories (9 percent from protein; 81 percent from carbohydrates; 10 percent from fat), 4 grams protein, 41 grams carbohydrates, 2 grams fat (less than 1 gram saturated fat), 27 milligrams cholesterol, 83 milligrams sodium*

Strawberry Shortcake

· ✳ ·

There's something undeniably comforting about strawberry short-cake. It's so, well, American, that it just puts me in the mood for a Fourth of July picnic and fireworks. This low-fat version will help you face the summer bathing suit, too. It's nice with a dollop of New "Whipped Cream" (page 138).

STRAWBERRIES
> **2 pints fresh strawberries, sliced, or 4 cups thawed**
>   **frozen strawberries, sliced**
> **3 tablespoons dark brown sugar**
>
> **Sarah's White Cake, unfrosted (page 122)**

1. In a medium bowl, toss the strawberries and brown sugar. Cover and refrigerate until the strawberries give off some juices, at least 2 hours or overnight.

2. To serve, cut the cake into twelve wedges. Using a slotted spoon, place equal amounts of the strawberries on individual dessert plates. Top with a cake wedge and drizzle with the strawberry juices.

Nutritional Analysis:
Per serving: *About 208 calories (6 percent from protein; 75 percent from carbohydrates; 20 percent from fat), 3 grams protein, 40 grams carbohydrates, 5 grams fat (3 grams saturated fat), 29 milligrams cholesterol, 99 milligrams sodium*

232 • The Healthy Oven Baking Book

Quick Fixes
from Mixes

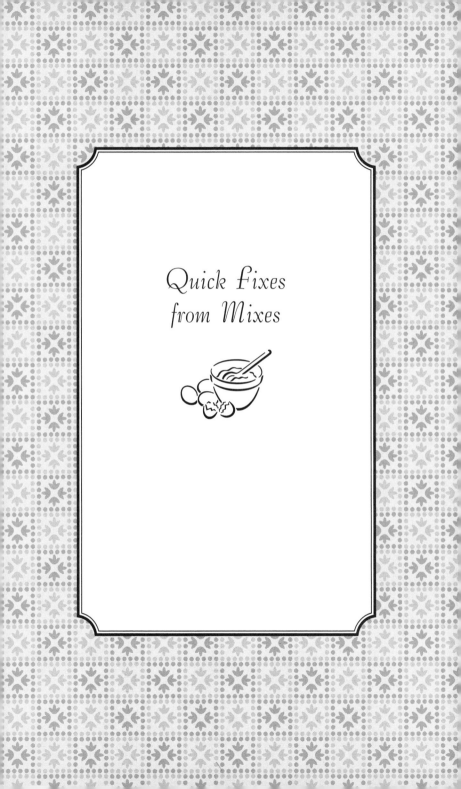

Apple-Raspberry Cobbler

MAKES 9 SERVINGS

· ✺ ·

H ere's a sweet-tart raspberry cobbler with an apple topping created from Healthy Oven's Apple Quick-Cake Mix. I always have a stash of frozen fruit in the freezer for turning into quick desserts, and while this is excellent with raspberries, I love it with blueberries or cherries, too, especially when topped with frozen yogurt.

Nonstick canola oil spray

RASPBERRIES
$1/2$ **cup water**
2 tablespoons sugar
1 tablespoon cornstarch
1 teaspoon vanilla extract
$1/4$ **teaspoon almond extract**
$1/2$ **teaspoon ground cinnamon**
2 cups fresh or frozen (do not thaw) raspberries

COBBLER
**One 8.8-ounce box Healthy Oven Low-Fat Apple
    Quick-Cake Mix***
$3/4$ **cup unsweetened applesauce**
$1/2$ **cup water**
1 tablespoon canola oil

1. To prepare the raspberries, in a medium saucepan, stir the water with the sugar, cornstarch, vanilla, almond extract, and cinnamon to dissolve the cornstarch. Cook over medium heat, stirring often, until boil-

*Includes (listed in order by weight): unbromated unbleached enriched wheat flour, brown sugar, dehydrated apple flakes, wheat bran, aluminum-free baking powder, dehydrated egg whites, nonfat dry milk, natural vanilla flavor, cinnamon, and salt.

ing. Stir in the raspberries. Set aside to cool completely. (The raspberry mixture will thicken as it cools.)

2. Position a rack in the center of the oven and preheat to 350° F. Lightly spray an 8 × 8-inch nonstick baking pan with oil. Spread the raspberry mixture in the prepared pan.

3. To make the cobbler, in a medium bowl, stir the cake mix, applesauce, water, and oil just until smooth. Do not overmix. Spoon the batter over the raspberries, covering the berries as much as possible (although some berries will show through).

4. Bake until the top of the cobbler springs back when pressed in the center, 20 to 25 minutes. Serve warm.

....

Nutritional Analysis:
Per serving: *About 141 calories (6 percent from protein; 83 percent from carbohydrates; 10 percent from fat), 2 grams protein, 30 grams carbohydrates, 2 grams fat (less than 1 gram saturated fat), 0 milligrams cholesterol, 182 milligrams sodium*

Upside-Down Nectarine Muffins

MAKES 6 MUFFINS

· ✷ ·

Y̶ou've heard of upside-down cake—well why not upside-down muffins? I love these with nectarines, which have an intensely fruity flavor, but peaches work well, too.

Nonstick canola oil spray

2 tablespoons packed dark brown sugar

2 ripe medium nectarines, unpeeled, pitted and thinly
  sliced

One 8.8-ounce box Healthy Oven Low-Fat Ginger
  Muffin Mix*

$^3/_4$ cup unsweetened applesauce

$^1/_3$ cup water

1 $^1/_2$ teaspoons canola oil

1. Position a rack in the center of the oven and preheat to 350° F. Lightly spray six 2 $^3/_4$ × 1 $^1/_2$-inch nonstick muffin cups with oil.

2. Sprinkle 1 teaspoon brown sugar into the bottom of each muffin tin, spreading the sugar as evenly as possible. Divide the sliced nectarines evenly over the sugar in the cups.

3. In a medium bowl, stir the muffin mix, applesauce, water, and oil just until combined. Do not overmix. Spoon equal amounts into the prepared muffin cups. Place the muffin tin on an aluminum foil–lined baking sheet to catch any bubbling sugar.

4. Bake until the tops of the muffins spring back when pressed in the center, 20 to 25 minutes. Do not overbake. Immediately run a sharp knife around the edges of the muffins to loosen them from the pan. Turn

---

*Includes (listed in order by weight): unbromated unbleached enriched wheat flour, brown sugar, cornstarch, wheat bran, aluminum-free baking powder, dehydrated egg whites, nonfat dry milk, all-natural spices, salt, and natural vanilla flavor.

the muffins out onto the baking sheet (be careful—the hot sugar may drip), Replace any stray nectarines. Let cool slightly before serving warm.

Nutritional Analysis:
Per muffin: *About 191 calories (7 percent from protein; 87 percent from carbohydrates; 6 percent from fat), 4 grams protein, 43 grams carbohydrates, 1 gram fat (less than 1 gram saturated fat), 0 milligrams cholesterol, 271 milligrams sodium*

Chocolate-Cherry Muffins

MAKES 6 MUFFINS

· ❋ ·

Chocolate and cherries are old friends. Dried cherries, available in both sweet and tart varieties, can be found at specialty food stores and in the produce section of many supermarkets. I prefer the tart cherries, but sweet will do, too.

Nonstick canola oil spray

**One 8.8-ounce box Healthy Oven Low-Fat Chocolate
    Muffin Mix***
³/₄ cup unsweetened applesauce
1 ¹/₂ teaspoons canola oil
¹/₃ cup water

¹/₂ cup dried tart cherries

1. Position a rack in the center of the oven and preheat to 350° F. Lightly spray six 2³/₄ × 1¹/₂-inch nonstick muffin cups with oil.

2. In a medium bowl, stir the muffin mix, applesauce, water, and oil just until combined (there should be a few traces of mix remaining). Add the cherries and stir just until the mix is incorporated. Do not overmix. Divide equally among the prepared muffin cups.

3. Bake until the tops of the muffins spring back when pressed in the center, 20 to 25 minutes. Do not overbake. Cool in the cups on a wire cake rack for 10 minutes before removing. Serve warm or at room temperature.

---

*Includes (listed in order by weight): unbromated unbleached enriched wheat flour, sugar, pure unsweetened chocolate (Dutch-process cocoa), wheat bran, aluminum-free baking powder, dehydrated egg whites, nonfat dry milk, salt, and natural vanilla flavor.

Nutritional Analysis:

Per muffin: *About 203 calories (6 percent calories from protein; 90 percent from carbohydrates; 4 percent from fat), 4 grams protein, 61 grams carbohydrates, 1 gram fat (0 grams saturated fat), 0 milligrams cholesterol, 281 milligrams sodium*

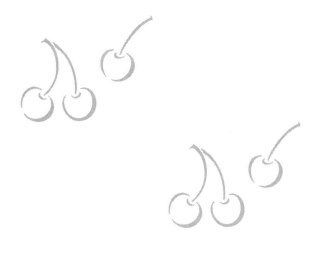

Quick Cinnamon Pancakes

MAKES 12 PANCAKES

· ❋ ·

When it comes to making pancakes, I am happy to say that many families have replaced their old all-purpose biscuit mix with Healthy Oven Muffin Mix. You can use any flavor, but I am partial to cinnamon. Of course, top your stack with maple syrup, honey, or fresh fruit.

Nonstick canola oil spray

One 8.8-ounce box Healthy Oven Low-Fat Cinnamon
    Muffin Mix*
1 ¼ cups water
2 teaspoons canola oil

1. Preheat a griddle or large skillet over medium-high heat until a splash of water sprinkled on the surface turns into tiny droplets.

2. Meanwhile, in a medium bowl, stir the muffin mix, water, and oil just until combined.

3. Spray griddle with oil. For each pancake, pour a scant ¼ cup of batter onto the hot griddle. Cook until tiny bubbles appear on the top and the edges look cooked, about 1 minute. Turn with a pancake turner and continue cooking until the underside is browned, about 1 more minute. Spray griddle in between each batch. Serve hot.

....

Nutritional Analysis:

Per pancake: *About 77 calories (8 percent from protein; 84 percent from carbohydrates; 9 percent from fat), 2 grams protein, 17 grams carbohydrates, 1 gram fat (0 grams saturated fat), 0 milligrams cholesterol, 136 milligrams sodium*

*Includes (listed in order by weight): Unbromated unbleached enriched wheat flour, brown sugar, cornstarch, wheat bran, aluminum-free baking powder, dehydrated egg whites, nonfat dry milk, salt, cinnamon, and natural vanilla flavor.

Fudge No-Fat Brownies

MAKES 9 BROWNIES

· ✻ ·

That's right—no fat. These chocolately treats show how well prune puree works in a baked chocolate dessert. If you wish, frost them with Vanilla Buttercream Frosting (page 136).

Nonstick canola oil spray

One 8.8-ounce box Healthy Oven Low-Fat Chocolate
    Quick-Cake Mix*

$^1\!/_2$ cup water

$^1\!/_2$ cup prune (or prune-fruit) baby food

$^1\!/_4$ cup applesauce

1. Position a rack in the center of the oven and preheat to 350° F. Lightly spray an 8 × 8-inch square nonstick baking pan with oil.

2. In a medium bowl, stir the cake mix, water, prune puree, and applesauce just until combined. Do not overmix. Spread into the prepared pan.

3. Bake until the top springs back when pressed gently in the center, 20 to 25 minutes. Do not overbake. Cool completely in the pan on a wire cake rack. To serve, cut into nine brownies.

....

Nutritional Analysis:

Per brownie: *About 112 calories (11 percent from protein; 89 percent from carbohydrates; 0 percent from fat), 3 grams protein, 24 grams carbohydrates, 0 grams fat (0 grams saturated fat), 0 milligrams cholesterol, 191 milligrams sodium*

*Includes (listed in order by weight): unbromated unbleached enriched wheat flour, sugar, pure unsweetened chocolate (Dutch-process cocoa), wheat bran, aluminum-free baking powder, dehydrated egg whites, nonfat dry milk, salt, and natural vanilla flavor.

Lemon-Cranberry Bars

MAKES 9 BARS

· ✳ ·

*T*hese can be decorated with a thin layer of Lemon Glaze (page 140). Otherwise, just dust them with a little confectioners' sugar, and enjoy them simple and unadorned.

Nonstick canola oil spray

One 8.8-ounce box Healthy Oven Low-Fat Lemon Quick-Cake Mix*

³/₄ cup unsweetened applesauce

¹/₂ cup water

¹/₂ cup fresh or frozen (do not thaw) cranberries

1. Position a rack in the center of the oven and preheat to 350° F. Lightly spray an 8 × 8-inch square nonstick baking pan with oil.

2. In a medium bowl, stir the cake mix, applesauce, and water just until combined (there should be a few traces of mix remaining). Add the cranberries and stir just until the mix is incorporated. Spread in the prepared pan.

3. Bake until the top springs back when pressed in the center, 20 to 25 minutes. Do not overbake. Cool completely in the pan on a wire cake rack. To serve, cut into nine bars.

....

Nutritional Analysis:

Per bar: About 102 calories (8 percent from protein; 92 percent from carbohydrates; 0 percent from fat), 2 grams protein, 25 grams carbohydrates, 0 grams fat (0 grams saturated fat), 0 milligrams cholesterol, 181 milligrams sodium.

*Includes (listed in order by weight): Unbromated unbleached enriched wheat flour, sugar, dehydrated apple flakes, wheat bran, aluminum-free baking powder, egg white powder, nonfat dry milk, natural flavors, salt, and lemon peel.

Citrus Poppy Seed Mini-Muffins

MAKES 18 MINI-MUFFINS

· ❋ ·

*M*ini-muffin tins can be found at any kitchenware shop. They make tiny muffins that kids just love. Keep an eye on them and don't overbake.

Nonstick canola oil spray

One 8.8-ounce box Healthy Oven Low-Fat Orange Muffin Mix*
³⁄₄ cup unsweetened applesauce
¹⁄₃ cup water
1 ¹⁄₂ teaspoons canola oil
2 tablespoons poppy seeds
Grated zest of 1 lemon or ¹⁄₄ teaspoon pure lemon oil

1. Position a rack in the center of the oven and preheat to 350° F. Lightly spray eighteen 1 ³⁄₄ × 1-inch nonstick mini-muffin cups with oil.

2. In a medium bowl, stir the muffin mix, applesauce, water, oil, poppy seeds, and lemon zest just until combined. Do not overmix. Divide equally among the prepared muffin cups.

3. Bake until the tops spring back when pressed in the center, 10 to 15 minutes. Do not overbake. Cool in the cups on a wire cake rack for 10 minutes before removing from the cups. Serve warm.

....

Nutritional Analysis:
Per mini-muffin: *About 63 calories (12 percent from protein; 80 percent from carbohydrates; 8 percent from fat), 1 gram protein, 12 grams carbohydrates, less than 1 gram fat (less than 1 gram saturated fat), 0 milligrams cholesterol, 94 milligrams sodium*

*Includes (listed in order by weight): Unbromated unbleached enriched wheat flour, sugar, cornstarch, wheat bran, aluminum-free baking powder, dehydrated egg whites, nonfat dry milk, salt, pure and natural flavors, and orange peel.

Chocolate-Pumpkin Marble Loaves

MAKES TWO 8 $^1/_2$ × 4 $^1/_2$-INCH LOAVES,
9 SERVINGS EACH

· ❊ ·

wo of my favorite flavors, pumpkin and chocolate, are combined to make a luscious pair of cakes just right for when you have to serve a bunch of hungry guests. Sometimes I give them a topping of Orange Buttercream Frosting (page 137). While most of the loaf recipes in this book use the standard 9 × 5-inch loaf pan, these use the slightly smaller 8 $^1/_2$ × 4 $^1/_2$-inch pans to accommodate the amount of batter made from the mixes. (If you use longer pans, the loaves will look flatter.)

Nonstick canola oil spray

CHOCOLATE BATTER
One 8.8-ounce box Healthy Oven Low-Fat Chocolate Quick-Cake Mix*
$^3/_4$ unsweetened applesauce
$^1/_2$ cup water
1 tablespoon canola oil

PUMPKIN BATTER
One 8.8-ounce box Healthy Oven Low-Fat Pumpkin Quick-Cake Mix†
$^3/_4$ cup unsweetened applesauce
$^1/_2$ cup water
1 tablespoon canola oil

*Includes (listed in order by weight): unbromated unbleached enriched wheat flour, sugar, pure unsweetened chocolate (Dutch-process cocoa), wheat bran, aluminum-free baking powder, dehydrated egg whites, nonfat dry milk, salt, and natural vanilla flavor.
†Includes (listed in order by weight): unbromated unbleached enriched wheat flour, brown sugar, sugar, dehydrated pumpkin flakes, wheat bran, aluminum-free baking powder, egg white powder, nonfat dry milk, natural flavors, salt, and orange peel.

1. Position a rack in the center of the oven and preheat to 350° F. Lightly spray two 8 ½ × 4 ½-inch nonstick loaf pans with oil. Line the bottom of each pan with waxed paper, and lightly spray again.

2. To make the chocolate batter, in a medium bowl, stir the chocolate cake mix, ¾ cup applesauce, ½ cup water, and 1 tablespoon oil just until combined. Do not overmix. Set aside.

3. To make the pumpkin batter, in another medium bowl, stir the pumpkin cake mix, ¾ cup applesauce, ½ cup water, and 1 tablespoon oil just until combined. Do not overmix.

4. Spoon about three fourths of the chocolate batter into the prepared pans, dividing the batter equally between the pans. Pour about three fourths of the pumpkin batter over the chocolate batter in the pans. Divide the remaining batter between the pans, using half chocolate and half pumpkin. Lightly swirl a table knife through the batters in each pan to make a marble pattern.

5. Bake until the top of the cakes springs back when pressed gently in the center, 30 to 35 minutes. If necessary, return them to the oven for an additional 5 minutes. Cool in the pans on a wire cake rack for 10 minutes. Unmold the cakes onto the rack and peel off the waxed paper. Turn right side up and let cool completely.

Nutritional Analysis:
Per serving: About 122 calories (11 percent calories from protein; 79 percent from carbohydrates; 10 percent from fat), 3 grams protein, 24 grams carbohydrates, 2 grams fat (less than 1 gram saturated fat), 0 milligrams cholesterol, 176 milligrams sodium

The Healthy Oven Pantry

sing the best ingredients is always the goal of a great cook, but it is even more important with reduced-fat baking, because there isn't the usual amount of butter to enhance and contribute flavor. Here is a glossary of the major ingredients used in this book. You will find every one of these ingredients in a well-stocked supermarket or natural food store. In a pinch, many can be mail-ordered from the sources on pages 259–60.

Flours, Grains, and Meals

Flour: This book uses wheat flour, even though flour can be milled from nuts, legumes, and some fruits and vegetables. The type of flour in a recipe is paramount. Also, it is extremely important to use a good quality flour. All flours are not alike—you can't switch from one type to another without wreaking havoc with your baked goods.

I much prefer flours milled from organically grown wheat—the flavor is superb and your desserts will be all the better for their use. I like the whole wheat pastry flour from Morgan's Mills (page 260) so much that I mail-order it to have on hand in my freezer at all times. I can also recommend Arrowhead Mills' whole grain pastry flour, which is carried by almost every natural food store and many supermarkets (it can also be mail-ordered from the sources on pages 259–60).

The brand of flour, be it whole wheat pastry or another variety, can affect the quality of your baked goods. I never really appreciated this until recently. I had run out of both Morgan's Mills and Arrowhead Mills flours, and decided to open a fresh bag of whole wheat pastry flour that I had mail-ordered from a well-known bakery catalogue. The cake did not bake well and was nowhere near as delicious as when it was made with my favorite flours. So, when you find a flour you like, stick with it.

I do not address substitutions for wheat flour for people with wheat allergies. These substitutions are very tricky, especially in low-fat cooking, and you should use only tested recipes from a wheat-free cookbook.

The natural oils found in whole grain flours, including cornmeal, make them susceptible to rancidity. Store all whole grain flours in plastic bags in the refrigerator or freezer. You can use it directly from the refrigerator or freezer. Store white flours in an airtight container in a cool, dark place.

Whole Wheat Flour: High-gluten, hard wheat flour, milled with the bran and germ. While I sometimes use it by itself, most often I mix it with unbleached all-purpose flour to give a better texture to baked goods.

Unbleached All-Purpose Flour: Flour made from a combination of soft and hard wheats with a moderate gluten content. The bran and germ have been removed, giving the flour an off-white color because it has not been chemically bleached. I tested these recipes with supermarket brands like General Mills and Pillsbury, but I have also used organic brands like Arrowhead Mills with much success.

Whole Wheat Pastry Flour: Low-gluten flour milled from soft wheat with the bran included. It is sometimes labeled Whole Grain Pastry Flour. *Do not confuse it with whole wheat flour.* Read each recipe carefully.

Cake Flour: Milled from soft white flour, this has a lower gluten content than whole wheat pastry flour. Do not use self-rising cake flour, which contains baking powder and salt. Cake flour is bleached to lighten its pale beige color. If you don't have cake flour on hand, make your own:

measure 1 cup all-purpose flour *minus* 2 tablespoons, and then add in 2 tablespoons cornstarch. Combine.

Wheat Products: I use *miller's wheat bran* (unprocessed bran flakes), a natural source of dietary fiber, found at natural food stores. It is less coarse than supermarket bran, and gives a better texture to baked goods, but you can use the supermarket variety if you wish. To add a nutty flavor without adding a lot of fat, I use *Grape-Nuts* cereal as a topping for some cakes.

Cornmeal: Use yellow, stone-ground cornmeal. It is available in bags at natural food stores and many supermarkets. Some cooks, especially those who live in the South, prefer white cornmeal as they believe it has a slightly sweeter flavor. The choice is up to you, but as a Northerner, I prefer yellow cornmeal.

Quick-Cooking Oats: The oat flakes in this type of oatmeal have been pressed more finely than old-fashioned, regular oats, and cook in a shorter time. Their fineness gives a nice oat taste without bulking up the dough, which can happen with regular oats. Don't use "instant" oats, which have been pressed even more finely.

Fruit Purees

Fruit purees are the most popular substitute for fat in healthful baking. While they are somewhat interchangeable, they have their own attributes. For example, prune puree's dark color may not be appropriate for a light-colored cake where applesauce would be a much better choice.

Unsweetened Applesauce: I always cook with a smooth, high-quality supermarket brand such as Mott's. I like its thick consistency, which is perfect for healthy baking. You can use other applesauces such as chunky, sliced, or cinnamon, cranberry, or raspberry, but I tested these recipes only with the smooth, unsweetened kind.

Prune Puree: This can now be found in jars at natural food stores and many supermarkets. Its rich flavor restricts its versatility, and I don't use it often in my recipes, but I mention it because it is a favorite of some cooks and food magazines. (It is most successful in chocolate desserts.)

Prune baby food, even though it may contain other fruits such as pears or apples, can be used in any recipe that calls for prune puree. I prefer baby food to the other prune purees that are sold as fat substitutes for baking.

Bananas: Mashed bananas are a great fat substitute, and lend flavor as well as bulk to the recipe. Use well-ripened bananas—they should be flecked with lots of brown spots, but not blackened. Mash bananas well with a fork so they retain a little texture, and don't blend them smooth in a blender.

Pumpkin: One of my favorite cooking ingredients. Even though autumn is considered the time to bake pumpkin desserts, I make them all year long. I prefer a high-quality, canned, solid pack pumpkin to freshly prepared pumpkin puree. Again, the quality and moisture content of canned is consistent, while freshly baked and pureed pumpkin can be much too watery for baking (although it makes wonderful soup). If you want to prepare your own pumpkin or winter squash puree, see the instructions on page 165.

Vegetable Oils

Most of these recipes use a bit of canola oil, which act as a flavor carrier, reduces stickiness, and help to retain flavors during the baking process. Remember, vegetable oil does not have the ability to create or hold air like creamed solid shortening with crystalline sugar, so eggs and other thick ingredients like fruit purees must do the job.

I use canola oil, but you can use any vegetable oil you prefer, except olive oil, which is more viscous and can impart its strong flavor to the baked goods. By the way, the canola plant does not exist. Canola oil is extracted from rapeseed, which is not a very attractive name. Most rapeseed is grown in Canada, whose government looked for a name that would make this excellent, monounsaturated oil more marketable. The result was an anagram for "Canada" and "oil": canola.

Dairy Products

Fresh dairy products, like low-fat milk, buttermilk, sour cream, cream cheese, and nonfat yogurt, are essential ingredients in reduced-fat baking. But I also cook with evaporated skimmed milk and instant dry non-fat milk powder to add special character to baked goods.

Low-Fat Milk: In testing these recipes, I used 1 percent low-fat milk. I always keep a box of shelf-stable milk (such as Parmalat) in my pantry for the times when I run out of milk and can't run to the market.

Low-Fat Buttermilk: An absolute must for people who love to bake! Buttermilk, like yogurt and sour cream, is an acidic ingredient, and helps tenderize the gluten formed in a batter. In addition to giving baked goods a tender texture, buttermilk also lends a rich tangy flavor. Buttermilk can vary in calories and fat grams according to the type of milk used to make it—I have seen types called nonfat, low-fat, light, and reduced-fat. All are interchangeable. However, all recipes in this book use low-fat buttermilk which is readily available in my area and the best one for reduced-fat baking. Most buttermilk these days is low-fat, but you may still find the regular variety, so be aware of the distinction. I want to encourage you to make it a staple in your cooking life, and always have a carton in the refrigerator for impromptu baking. Shake the carton before using. I prefer fresh buttermilk to instant buttermilk powder which reconstitutes into a thin liquid. When I run out of buttermilk, I make my own low-fat variety. For one cup: place 1 tablespoon freshly distilled white vinegar (does not add flavor to a baked good) in a glass measuring cup. Add in 1 percent milk to equal 1 cup. Stir. Let stand for 5 minutes until milk is thickened and curdled. Or, use ²/₃ cup plain nonfat or low-fat yogurt plus ¹/₃ cup 1 percent milk to equal 1 cup buttermilk. Use either as directed.

Nonfat Yogurt: Another staple that I have in my refrigerator. I prefer organic, acidophilus brands like Stonyfield Farms, without stabilizers or gelatins. Fruit-flavored yogurts can be used to flavor baked goods (see the Apricot Corn Cake on page 58).

Yogurt Cheese: This isn't a product that you can buy in the store (yet), but simply yogurt that has had the whey drained off. It's easy to do. Line a wire strainer with paper towels or cheesecloth, and place it over a deep, medium-size bowl. Be sure the bottom of the strainer clears the bottom of the bowl by 2 or 3 inches. Spoon four cups (one thirty-two-ounce container) plain nonfat yogurt into the strainer and place a paper towel or more cheesecloth on top. Place a saucer or small plate in the strainer to lightly weight the yogurt. Let stand in the refrigerator until about two cups of the whey has drained off, and the yogurt is thick and somewhat firm, about one and a half hours. (There are also yogurt cheese making contraptions that are available at kitchenware shops.) If you hate to discard the tangy whey, some frugal cooks use it in soups— but do not use it as a substitute for the liquids in a baked recipe. If you're not in a hurry, do not weight the yogurt with the saucer, and refrigerate the whole setup overnight to slowly drain the whey. *The yogurt cheese will yield about half the volume of the undrained yogurt: for example, four cups of yogurt (one thirty-two-ounce container) will yield about two cups of yogurt cheese.*

Reduced-Fat Sour Cream: Use this instead of nonfat sour cream, because the fat content and acidity differ between the two and the taste and texture will be better.

Neufchâtel Cream Cheese: This has one-third the fat of regular cream cheese, and can be found in the refrigerated sections of all supermarkets. Nonfat cream cheeses do not work as well as Neufchâtel in baked desserts.

Stick Butter: My favorite supermarket brand is Land O Lakes. All brands of butter do *not* taste alike and the texture can be different, too. I use unsalted (sometimes called sweet, stick) butter so that I can control the amount of salt in the recipe. Also, butter is salted to increase its shelf life and to hide any off flavors, so unsalted butter tends to be fresher and better tasting. Since butter is used more as a flavoring than as a shortener in reduced-fat baking, it should be the best you can find. Do not use "whipped" tub butter, only stick butter, which I freeze in airtight plastic bags to retain freshness.

I know that some bakers may be concerned about the saturated fat in butter, but keep in mind that these recipes call for less butter than traditional recipes. However, I want to warn against using margarine as a substitute. Margarine does not have the same flavor and texture as butter, and it really doesn't contribute to the final flavor of a baked good. If you need a butter substitute, use a butter/margarine blend, such as Land O Lakes Country Morning (in sticks, not whipped or tub versions).

Instant Nonfat Dry Milk Powder: This is included in some batters to add structure and flavor without adding fat or moisture. Use the instant milk powder *dry,* as specified in the recipes—do not reconstitute.

Evaporated Skimmed Milk: A canned product, this is a reduced-fat version of regular evaporated milk. Because it is thicker than milk, it can be used to simulate cream in doughs and batters. It can also be heated, mixed with sugar and gelatin, chilled, and beaten into a more-than-acceptable substitute for whipped cream (see New "Whipped Cream," page 138). Store canned milk in a dark, cool place, where it will keep up to 2 years.

Low-Fat Sweetened Condensed Milk: In its regular, high-fat version, this canned milk is a traditional ingredient in Key lime recipes. It is a good example of how many familiar products are being given healthier, reduced-fat profiles. It is much thicker than evaporated skimmed milk and very sweet. I use it in recipes like the Florida Lime Bars on page 200.

Eggs

Eggs are the backbone of many baked goods. Egg yolks add moisturizing fat and help emulsify the batter, and egg whites act as strengtheners. Some low-fat bakers eliminate egg yolks from their baked goods, and bake with all whites. I find that this makes rubbery cakes, muffins, and cookies. You need the lecithin in the yolk as a emulsifier. If you like liquid egg substitute, you can use it according to the manufacturer's directions, but I much prefer natural eggs.

Size: Always bake with grade A large eggs. The size of the eggs is important, as medium eggs yield a drier baked good.

Note: Eggs should always be stored in the interior of the refrigerator, but some books say that room temperature egg whites beat to the highest fluffiest peaks. To quickly bring up the egg's temperature for meringue-based desserts, place the uncracked eggs in a bowl of hot tap water for 5 minutes—they will be at the perfect temperature for beating the egg whites to stiff peaks. Do not overbeat. Crack and separate the eggs, placing the egg whites into a clean, dry bowl. Do not have a trace of egg yolk remaining. However, in separating warm eggs, the yolks break more easily. Thus, I always whip egg whites from eggs right from the refrigerator; my recipes always turn out just fine.

In preparing the recipes, you may have left-over egg whites or yolks. Here's what I do with mine:

1. I keep extra egg whites in the refrigerator, tightly covered. I also freeze them. To freeze, place egg whites in a Pyrex custard cup, tightly covered. To thaw, let the egg whites stand at room temperature.

2. Keep extra egg yolks covered in an airtight plastic container, in the freezer. Before freezing, mix each yolk with $1/4$ teaspoon of sugar. To thaw, let them stand at room temperature, and then mix well. They will not look the same as fresh egg yolks do, but they work just as well.

Two dried egg white products, *dried egg white powder* and *meringue powder,* are very useful in low-fat baking. They are both available at kitchenware and cake decorating shops, bakery suppliers, some supermarkets, and by mail-order.

Pasteurized Dried Egg White Powder: When I separate eggs to use the whites in a recipe, I always have left-over yolks. So, I always have dried egg white powder in the house. It's easy to use—just follow the manufacturer's instructions. Be sure to stir the powder well to reconstitute it.

Meringue Powder: When I created low-fat frosting recipes for this book (pages 134 and 136), meringue powder (dried egg whites with sugar, cream of tartar, and cornstarch) saved the day—it easily stabilized the frosting like no other ingredient. Meringue powder like dried egg whites, is pasteurized and completely safe from harmful bacteria.

Sweeteners

Granulated and confectioners' sugar are staples in just about everyone's kitchen, so there's no need to go into much detail here. Except for one important thing: If you want your reduced-fat desserts to have traditional flavor and texture, there is no substitute for good old sugar. Here are some other sweeteners that you may not use as often.

Brown Sugar: I prefer the richer flavor of dark brown sugar to light. When I say brown sugar, I use the sticky, damp kind, not raw brown sugar crystals (like Sugar in the Raw) or a free-flowing dry brown sugar called "Brownulated." Measure brown sugar by packing it into a metal measuring cup with a spoon and leveling the top.

Corn Syrup: Adds moisture as well as a mellow sweetness to recipes. Use light corn syrup, not dark.

Molasses: A by-product of sugar production, molasses comes in mild (unsulphured), robust (processed with sulfites), and blackstrap versions. I always use mild unsulphured molasses. Don't use blackstrap molasses, which is too strong and doesn't work well in my recipes.

Pure Maple Syrup: Most pure maple syrup is grade A amber, which is delicious on its own, and can be best appreciated on pancakes and waffles. It is always pricey, as this natural food is subject to variations in annual harvesting conditions. Pure maple syrup has a much lighter flavor than supermarket pancake syrup, which is corn syrup with artificial maple flavors. Natural maple syrup works well as a sweetener, but it really doesn't impart a deep maple flavor in baked goods. There are two options to increase the maple flavor. The first is to use grade B maple syrup, which is available by mail-order. Or, add a few drops of natural maple flavoring extract to the grade A syrup.

Honey: Honey is another liquid sweetener. My recipe for Honey Snack Cake (page 74) shows honey at its best. Use a full-flavored honey, such as wildflower.

Fruit Juices: For the best results, use freshly squeezed fruit juices in baking (besides, you'll have the grated zest to add for even more flavor). Some recipes call for fruit juice concentrates. You can use the familiar frozen fruit juice concentrate (thaw before using), or the new shelf-stable variety. Do not dilute fruit juice concentrates.

Flavorings

These are the ingredients that add distinction and character to baked goods. Imagine how dull desserts would be without chocolate or vanilla, lemon or coffee, cinnamon or nutmeg.

Salt: An essential baking element, it also plays an important role in regulating our body's fluids and blood pressure. I add the minimum amount of salt to enhance the flavor of a recipe. I use iodized table salt, which dissolves easily and has a clean flavor.

Chocolate and Cocoa: When cocoa beans are roasted and ground, they can be mixed with other ingredients to create chocolate, or processed into dry cocoa powder. It may surprise you to find that 1 ounce of cocoa powder contains only 3 grams of fat, while the same amount of unsweetened chocolate has 15 grams.

Practically every baker knows regular cocoa, usually found in a familiar brown box, but I use only *Dutch-process cocoa powder*. Dutch-process cocoa powder is treated with alkali. This treatment reduces the cocoa's acidity, darkens and reddens its color, and smoothes its flavor. (The process was invented in The Netherlands in the early 1800s.) There are American alkali-process cocoas on the market, but they may be hard to identify by the label (Hershey's version is in a silver box and called "European-Style.") Look at the nutritional label to see if the ingredients include "alkali," and if they do, you've found a Dutch-process cocoa. Regular and Dutch-process cocoas are not always interchangeable, as the flavor and color aren't the same, and may require different types of leavenings.

Bittersweet chocolate is usually European, but there are some American versions. Do not confuse it with unsweetened chocolate, which has no sugar at all. Professional quality bittersweet chocolate is now available at specialty food stores. Keep in mind that some of those varieties are *very* bitter, and are not to everyone's taste. (Usually, the higher the percentage of cocoa solids listed on the package, the more bitter the chocolate. A 70 percent cocoa solids chocolate is pretty bitter, and few kids will like it.) I like Baker's and Hershey's bittersweet chocolate, found in grocery stores. Semisweet chocolate, although somewhat sweeter, can be substituted for bittersweet.

Chocolate burns easily, so be careful when melting it. My favorite way to melt chocolate is the way my mom taught me. Place the unchopped square of chocolate on a piece of aluminum foil and put it in the oven while it is preheating. It will take about ten minutes for the chocolate to melt—check it often and press it with your finger to gauge its progress. If you want to speed the process, chop the chocolate in even pieces and place it on the foil. When the chocolate has melted, let it cool until tepid and scrape it into the batter with a rubber spatula.

Chocolate can also be melted in a microwave oven. Place one ounce or more of finely chopped chocolate in a microwave-safe bowl, and microwave on Medium (50 percent) checking occasionally until the chocolate looks shiny (it won't look melted), two to four minutes, depending on the brand. Let stand for thirty seconds or so, then stir to see if it is melted enough.

The classic way to melt chocolate is in the top part of a double boiler over very hot, but not simmering water. Sometimes it is more efficient to put the finely chopped chocolate in a small heatproof bowl and place over a small saucepan of water. In any case, be sure that no water comes in contact with the chocolate, or it will firm up or "seize."

Instant Espresso Powder: Coffee compliments the flavor of chocolate. Instant espresso powder can be found in Italian delicatessens and many supermarkets. The most common brand is Medaglia d'Oro, but brands from major American companies are coming onto the market in reaction to our newfound love for "real" coffee. If you wish, you can substitute regular instant coffee, but it isn't nearly as intensely flavored.

Extracts: Use only the best, naturally flavored pure extracts. My favorite is Nielsen-Massey Madagascar Bourbon Vanilla, which can be found at specialty food stores and many kitchenware shops.

Citrus Zests and Oils: With just a few movements of the grater, you can add fragrant citrus zest to your batter (I prefer using organic citrus for its superior flavor). But wash and dry the fruit carefully before grating it. When grating the zest, be sure to use only the colored part of the peel, don't grate into the bitter white pith underneath it. Use a dry pastry brush to remove any zest that clings to the grater.

When I don't have fresh citrus handy, I use pure citrus oils from Boyajian instead (see Mail-Order Sources, page 259). These are powerful natural essences cold pressed from citrus rinds. They come in orange, lime, or lemon flavors. Don't confuse them with citrus-flavored salad oils. In baking, I often substitute one-quarter teaspoon pure citrus oil for the grated zest of one fresh fruit—the citrus oils actually have a more intense flavor than the fresh zest. Do not increase the amounts specified in the recipes. To store the oil, wrap the bottle in aluminum foil and refrigerate it—sunlight and warm temperatures can reduce the oil's flavor.

Spices: Keep your spices fresh by storing them in a cool, dark place, never near a warm stove. Discard any unused spices after six months—stale spices lose their flavor. It's a good idea to mark the purchase date on the label. I love cinnamon, but it is too difficult to grind fresh. Just purchase a high-quality brand. On the other hand, freshly grated nutmeg is easy to prepare, either with a small nutmeg grater or using the smallest holes of a cheese grater. It is so much more fragrant than bottled ground nutmeg.

Nuts and Seeds: These are used sparingly in reduced-fat baking—they may be flavorful, but they can also rack up a lot of fat grams. (If you want to delete them from a recipe, go ahead.) Nuts and seeds contain oils that can easily go rancid. To store them, wrap airtight and keep in the freezer.

Mail-Order Sources

Healthy Oven, Inc.
9 Newton Court
Croton-on-Hudson, NY 10520
(800) 7-LOW-FAT (756-9328)
Web Site:
http://www.healthyoven.com
E-Mail: healthyovn@aol.com
Healthy Oven Low-Fat Baking
Mixes, free recipes and catalogue.
Also, subscriptions to Sarah's
Healthy Oven Newsletter and
Recipe Club.

Arrowhead Mills
Box 2059
Hereford, TX 79045
(800) 749-0730
Organically grown flours.

Boyajian, Inc.
349 Lennox Street

Norwood, MA 02062
(781) 440-9500
Manufacturer of pure citrus oil and
other flavoring oils.

Deb-El Egg Whites
2 Papetti Plaze
Elizabeth, NJ 07206
(908) 351-0330
Dried egg white powder.

The King Arthur Flour Baker's
Catalog
P.O. Box 876
Norwich, VT 05055-0876
(800) 827-6836
Excellent one-stop shopping for
baking supplies: meringue powder,
egg white powder, pure citrus oils,
assorted flours (unfortunately, I
don't recommend their whole wheat

pastry flour), nonstick baking utensils, and dried fruits.

Morgan's Mills
168 Payson Rd
Union, ME 04862
(207) 785-4900
Organically grown flours, especially whole wheat pastry flour.

Morse Farm
Country Road
Montpelier, VT 05602
(802) 223-2740
Pure maple syrup (also has full-flavored grade B, which is best for baking).

Nordic Ware
Highway 7 & 100
Minneapolis, MN 55416
(612)-920-2888 ext 629
Bundt and Bundtlette pans

Penzeys Spices
P.O. Box 1448
Waukesha, WI 53187
(414) 574-0277
High-quality spices and extracts.

Vanns Spices Ltd
1238 E. Joppa Rd
Baltimore, MD 21286
(410) 583-1643
High-quality spices and extracts.

Walnut Acres Organic Farms
Walnut Acres Road
Penns Creek, PA 17862
(800) 433-3998
Organically grown flours and dried fruits.

Williams-Sonoma
Mail-Order Department
P.O. Box 7456
San Francisco, CA 94120
(800) 541-2233
Baking utensils, pure citrus oils, pure extracts, and meringue powder.

Index